The Pleasure of Her Text

FEMINIST READINGS OF BIBLICAL & HISTORICAL TEXTS

The Pleasure
of Her Text

Feminist Readings of
Biblical & Historical Texts

Edited by
Alice Bach

Trinity Press International
Philadelphia

First published 1990

Trinity Press International
3725 Chestnut Street
Philadelphia, PA 19104

Library of Congress Cataloging-in-Publication Data

The Pleasure of her text: feminist readings of Biblical &
    historical texts/edited by Alice Bach.
        p.   cm.
    ISBN 0-334-02479-X
    1. Women in the Bible. 2. Women and religion. I. Bach,
    Alice.
BS575.P55   1990
220.6'082--dc20   90-40831

Printed in the U.S.A.

Contents

A Word of Thanks

THE CONTRIBUTIONS IN this volume originally appeared in *Union Seminary Quarterly Review* (*USQR*). This publication is among a handful of scholarly journals edited entirely by doctoral students. Although *USQR* has a Faculty Advisory Board of distinguished scholars representing many aspects of biblical and theological endeavor, the editorial policies, subject matter of each issue, and editing and management of the journal rest with its student editors. It has been my great pleasure to serve as editor for the past two years. I am grateful to Union Seminary for the freedom to offer scholars the latitude to experiment with method and voice in the articles they submit to *USQR*. Rarely does an editor have such an opportunity: to offer varied thematic issues and multiple points of view in one journal. The diversity of opinions in *USQR* reflects the diversity of Union itself.

During my editorship, I have been fortunate in having Gary Gilbert as the managing editor. He has waved his organizational wand at many crucial points, proving himself a wizard amid details and deadlines. The other student editors must be acknowledged for their time and skills. They know the importance of their contributions in evaluating articles. Harold Rast, editor of Trinity Press International, is truly an editor's editor. His wit and guidance were an invaluable help in selecting the articles that comprise *The Pleasure of Her Text*.

Introduction

THE QUESTION OF how feminism should define itself in relation to other critical methods and theories has caused sharp debate both in Europe and the U.S.A. As Judith Fetterley declared in *The Resisting Reader,* feminist criticism has been characterized by a resistance to codification and a refusal to have its parameters prematurely set. At this time most feminists agree that there are many communities of women, crucial differences *within* the category of women, and most important, there is no single message of feminist hermeneutics.

Gender is a word that heralds both risks and resistance. The resistance comes usually from those who have never thought of gender as influencing reading. The male gender has dominated the voice of the text, including also its interpretative voice, for such a long time that it is considered normative, objective, usual. "Objectivity is really male subjectivity," to use Adrienne Rich's aphorism. As we have noted, the gender code in the interpretation of biblical texts has usually been adopted in its masculine version. But each time the canon is termed universal, the life of the patriarchal myth is extended. When the gender code is implicit, it contains the same characteristics as the moral code. It imposes upon every signifying element of the text a unified and preestablished theme. Only since the development of women's studies has the gender code been explicitly criticized and explicitly embraced—in its *feminist* version. If feminist criticism has demonstrated anything, it has demonstrated the importance of the reader to what is read.

Of course feminists are products of the patriarchal culture too, and so have to deny the temptation of trying to produce a universal truth, a univocal meaning. Feminist criticism must remain fluid, not fixed, so that each one of us can contend with the ripples and waves of the dominant culture, diving into language to recover everything that is duplicitous and resistant and confounding. Elaine Showalter in a recent article has called for feminists to insist upon the recognition that gender is a central problem in every text, read or taught, whatever the era and whoever the author. A central problem, yes. But surely there are major risks in focusing on gender, splitting the world of reader into two. The first risk is reductiveness, to lose sight of the fact that focusing on certain categories obscures individual variation. Proclaiming *the* feminist agenda glosses over each woman's struggle for self-definition. Rather than locking people into categories, feminist literary critics need to form temporary alliances and coalitions. Shifting boundaries of sexual difference must not be prevented from shifting. It is the desire to remain fluid, not fixed, to encourage spontaneity instead of linear argumentation, that inspired this volume. A large part of the *pleasure* of the text is the sense of process, of moving along a road toward feminism, a term which refuses definition or categorization.

In her chapter "Protestant Feminists and the Bible," Mary Ann Tolbert illuminates general characteristics of the Protestant tradition that are barriers for many women in appropriating a considerable amount of recent feminist research. Protestant feminists, Tolbert argues, experience special problems (not encountered by Catholic or Jewish feminists) specifically related to the Protestant tradition, the diversity of Protestant denominations one of the most evident. A primary problem, the ramification of *sola scriptura* for feminists, is that Protestant feminists have difficulty dispensing with the authority of scripture in favor of historical reconstruction. Tolbert calls for feminist literary critics to raise the issue of gender, to read with suspicion against the "male as norm" convention of reading biblical texts. Tolbert's article begins the book because it raises the basic issues that concern each of the contributors: the question of gender and sexual difference in our scholarly lives.

Feminist literary critics are now examining the role of woman in biblical texts as enabler of the patriarchal society. In "The Pleasure of Her Text," I have offered a rereading of the story of Abigail, the prototypical good wife. While interpreters have always praised her, I wondered why, if Abigail was so good, she wasn't rewarded with a son who became king? What I learned is that women have moments of strong speech and proud action in male-centered biblical narratives, but strong independent women act at the pleasure of their male creators. Too forceful and they embody male fears, and must be silenced or written out of the narrative.

Cheryl Exum protests the marginalization of female biblical characters through analysis of the phallogocentric texts in which they appear. Her chapter, "Murder They Wrote," examines the silencing of female characters by their male creators. Punishing a woman like Michal, who speaks her mind with barrenness and silence (narrative death), is one sort of message to women readers. Another patriarchal message is to glorify the obedient daughter who sacrifices her own life to help her father keep a vow to God. According to the biblical text, this model daughter is remembered in song each year by other obedient daughters. Exum demonstrates that we can choose to read the story of Jephthah's daughter differently, "to expose the valorization of submission and glorification of the victim as serving phallocentric interests and to redefine its images of female solidarity in an act of feminist symbol-making."

Female scholars working with historical texts are confronted with a problem similar to that of their literary colleagues: they are reading the female voice as a palimpsest through the script of the dominant narrative. The texts that concern Carole Fontaine in her chapter, "A Heifer from Thy Stable," come from ancient Near Eastern societies: Mesopotamia and Anatolia. One of Fontaine's major concerns is whether patriarchal texts can speak the reality of women's lives. Fontaine searches for a model to evaluate the status of ancient women and the relationship of that status to the presence of goddesses and their worship. While Fontaine is faced with methodological considerations, she is attuned to the voices of these long-forgotten women. Never losing the thread of the women themselves to the temptation of scholarly method, Fontaine listens to the past. In their own words ancient women reflect the strength and wit with which they addressed and expanded the roles decreed for them by society.

Ellen Ross wonders what use feminist theologians have for a concept that characterizes human persons as imitators of a God who is often portrayed as a male deity. By creating a dialogue between two medieval theologians of the Augustinian tradition and two feminist theologians, Rosemary Ruether and Dorothee Soelle, Ross suggests that the heritage of the concept of *imago dei* may yet offer guidance to contemporary communities of renewal and hope. Ross's exploration points to the role of feminist theology in recognizing the implications of the image of God theme for shaping our political experience "insofar as theological claims have praxis implications that call for concrete responses."

Martha Reineke looks at an important time of women's history, the witch hunts of 1450–1750. In "The Devils Are Come Down Upon Us," she sets out to redress the Reformation historians' neglect of this period of victimization of and violence against women. Through a synthesis of methodologies, especially the work of René Girard, she

challenges other scholars in religious studies to refocus current
strategies of analysis in order to be more responsive to the charge of
feminist history. Reineke argues that "we seriously underestimate
the resources of our discipline at a point where they are most crucial
for our work *in memoriam* on behalf of our foresisters. To speak
adequately of the witch craze, to remember all that we must remember if we are to free our foresisters from a history of victimization, we
must treat myth as essential to the witch craze and its violence."

For some female scholars devising a new voice as well as new
methodologies in which to cast their ideas is a way of deconstructing
the patriarchal mold. Thus genre becomes a means to a political statement. While I am not suggesting that all female scholars search for
a new means of written expression, or even that such a universal
search would be desirable, let us consider some questions that Luce
Irigaray has raised: "What other mode of reading or writing or interpretation and affirmation may be mine inasmuch as I am a woman,
with respect to you, a man? Is it possible that the difference might *not*
be reduced once again to a process of hierarchization? Of sub-
ordinating the other to the same?" Based on a corporeality of
difference, writers such as Irigaray and Helene Cixous attempt to
dislodge the primacy of the phallogocentric binary opposition of
sameness by breaking down the hierarchy of presence/lack, or what
Irigaray calls the "old dream of symmetry." In the "new" syntax, as
she imagines it, "there would no longer be either subject or object,
'oneness' would no longer be privileged. . . . Instead the syntax
would involve proximity that would preclude any establishment of
ownership, thus any form of appropriation."

Whatever forms are constructed, the important element is to appropriate a nonhierarchical articulation of sexual difference in
language. However, a language of universal gynocentrism is not the
answer. Women do not share the same cultural and social conditions.
Feminist writing should be resistant to sameness, to speaking someone else's language, even if that language imitates other feminist
scholars. Cultural and racial differences are often first noticed (and
first submerged) in language. Women must take the initiative in
preserving the particularity of their own language. And feminists
will have to work to assure diversity of language in scholarly publica-
tions. Women in all scholarly disciplines will have to work together
to assure diversity—to bring pleasure to the text.

ALICE BACH
New York City
June 1990

did jesus have a baby sister?

dory previn
Southfield, Massachusetts

did jesus have a baby sister?
was she bitter?
was she sweet?
did she wind up in a convent?
did she end up on the street?
on the run?
on the stage?
did she dance?
did he have a sister?
a little baby sister?
did jesus have a sister?
did they give her a chance?

did he have a baby sister?
could she speak out
by and large?
or was she told by mother mary
ask your brother he's in charge
he's the whipped cream
on the cake
did he have a sister?
a little baby sister?
did jesus have a sister?
did they give her a break?

her brother's
birth announcement
was pretty big
pretty big
i guess
while she got precious
little notice
in the local press
her mother was the virgin
when she carried him
carried him
therein

if the little girl came later
then
was she conceived in sin?
and in sorrow?
and in shame?
did jesus have a sister?
what was her name?

did she long to be the savior
saving everyone
she met?
and in private to her mirror
did she whisper
saviorette?
saviorwoman?
saviorperson?
save your breath!
did he have a sister?
a little baby sister?
did jesus have a sister?
was she there at his death?

and did she cry for mary's comfort
as she watched him
on the cross?
and was mary too despairing
ask your brother
he's the boss
he's the chief
he's the man
he's the show
did he have a sister?
a little baby sister?
did jesus have a sister?
doesn't anyone know?

Protestant Feminists and the Bible: On the Horns of a Dilemma

MARY ANN TOLBERT
Vanderbilt University Divinity School

FOR MANY WOMEN the freedom to proclaim their own experience in the world and their own vision of the world as authoritative and legitimate, rather than marginal and deviant as patriarchy would have it, is the profoundly liberating dynamic of the feminist movement. However, for many feminists, and especially for many Jewish and Christian feminists, their own experience is often painfully split within itself because, to echo Elaine Showalter's words,[1] we are both the daughters of the male tradition, of Abraham and the patriarchs, of Jesus, Paul, and the Church Fathers, of our male ministers and rabbis, professors and dissertation advisors, and at the same time sisters together in a new consciousness, which rejects the submissive, victimized roles Western society, formed and molded by these two great religious traditions, has forced us, and generations of our foremothers and sisters, to play. Consciousness of the mutilation of minds, spirits, and bodies perpetrated for centuries on women by patriarchal misogyny demands not only our rage but also our absolute commitment to oppose and dismantle all the societal structures still supporting that misogyny. We cannot will away this new consciousness no matter how much discomfort it sometimes causes in our personal and professional lives. We can no longer teach or preach male history, androcentric ethics, or patriarchal biblical interpretations as though they were universals; we can no longer pledge unquestioning allegiance to existing religious hierarchies and institutions as though they actually served the whole family of Mother God rather than mainly the brethren. We cannot forget what we as feminists now know, any more than we can deny the degree to which patriarchal patterns continue to shape our lives and careers, either through our acceptance of them or through our rebellion against them.

This split within our experience, being both the heirs and the victims of patriarchy, is nowhere more apparent than in many women's struggles to come to terms with the religious traditions in which they were born, raised, or formed. Short of throwing out whole traditions and developing entirely new religious systems, an option I believe all feminists must leave open, is it possible for feminists to extract the gold, silver, and clothing out of their religious lands of slavery without also keeping the manacles and chains, just as the children of Israel were successful in doing with Egypt (Exod 12:35–36)? In this essay I wish to explore that question specifically in relation to the struggles of women in one particular strand of the Christian tradition: Protestantism. I have chosen this group not only because it is the one I know best, having been myself raised in a Protestant denomination and having taught for the past nine years in a nondenominational, primarily Protestant divinity school but also because I believe that Protestant feminists encounter special problems related to their tradition that have not been analyzed sufficiently for their similarities and differences with feminists from other Christian and Jewish traditions to become clear, and such clarity may let us understand each other better and thus help each other more. This essay is only as an initial attempt at assessing these issues and, hence, in no way pretends to be a final or full explication.

The specific experience which inaugurated my thinking on this subject was the observation that many of my Protestant women students find difficulty in appropriating much current feminist biblical research and proposals for Women-Church or the *ekklēsia* of women.[2] They certainly comprehend the issues and are indeed eager to learn of and investigate the fuller, more central role of women in early Christian history, as feminist reconstructions are uncovering it. The difficulty arises, however, in drawing from such studies a definite *praxis* for them. There appears, in other words, to be some lack of fit between these feminist writings and their own concrete experiences. Since feminism, like all liberation movements, should always result in *praxis*, for the point is to *change the world*, not simply add to our knowledge about it, this difficulty in appropriation is in need of analysis and explanation.

In conversations, both formal and informal, with groups of students over the last two years, three general characteristics of the Protestant tradition consistently surface as barriers for many women in appropriating a considerable amount of recent feminist research. I would like to list and explain the problems caused by each characteristic briefly and then devote the remainder of this essay to a fuller exploration of the first, the role of scripture in Protestantism.

Problems in the Protestant Tradition

From the time of Martin Luther's defense before the Diet of Worms in 1521, the first principle guiding the Protestant Reformation and the various groups growing out of it was the conviction of *sola scriptura*: "Scripture alone is the true over-lord and master of all writings and doctrines on earth."[3] Although feminists cannot help but notice the patriarchal language by which Luther articulated this doctrine, the primacy granted to scripture and its authority over all human ideas, structures, decisions, and theologies continues to be one of the most potent influences in the religious formation of anyone raised in the Protestant tradition. While I intend to return to this principle and its ramifications for feminists later, even on a simple reading of it the reason why some Protestant feminists have difficulty dispensing with the text of scripture in favor of historical reconstructions becomes more evident.

The second characteristic of modern Protestantism that poses major problems for feminists is its striking diversity. One cannot speak of a Protestant view or position on anything; rather one encounters many views. Even the various denominations tend often to be split into several factions, so that, for example, one cannot talk about *the* Lutheran position but must say the Missouri Synod Lutheran position. This diversity is found not only in dogma and tradition but also in liturgy, church organization, and denominational structure. Such pervasive diversity tends to isolate Protestant feminists from each other, and women's isolation from other women has always been one of the best weapons of patriarchal oppression: divide and conquer. Protestant women attempting to worship together, for instance, must begin by deciding whose order of worship to follow, whose hymnal to use, and whose liturgy to enact, so that our celebrations of sisterhood end up emphasizing our lives of separation. The actual number of feminists throughout all the Protestant denominations would prove, I believe, to be a substantial and highly influential body, but by dividing that body into separate groups of Methodist women, Presbyterian women, Disciples women,

Baptist women, etc., and pitting each group against frustratingly different androcentric denominational structures, the numbers and influence of Protestant feminists have often been successfully marginalized. Indeed, so serious are the many differences in denominational structures and politics that Protestant feminists often do not even understand what their sisters in other denominations are facing and thus do not know how to support or help them. In such a situation, ideas of Women-Church or the *ekklēsia* of women involve the visionary power of a longed-for "new Jerusalem"; yet, attempts to enact that vision tend only to underscore the reality of competing Protestant traditions that block unity.

Perversely enough, what little unity Protestant women were able to forge in the late sixties and early seventies in quest of the right of ordination in a number of denominations was quickly eroded by the very success of that campaign. Ordination itself has now become one more line of division among Protestant women, and one, I think, of the most dangerous, for it has the possibility of co-opting women into an androcentric hierarchical power structure rather than changing that structure.[4] The difference in power, status, and authority between clergy and laity in most Protestant denominations is arguably one of the clearest examples of patriarchal patterning in the social organization of Christianity. Priests and ministers stand over their congregations as fathers over children, shepherds over sheep, holy people over secular people, in an obvious dominant-subordinate relationship. Some denominations, in fact, formalize this gulf between clergy and laity by enrolling clergy, not in the membership of the churches they serve, but rather in the area association of other clergy.[5] Hence, the "church" for clergy are other clergy.

In past years many feminists hoped that as more women were ordained and filled parish posts, a different, more egalitarian model of ministry would emerge. So far, such has not proved to be the case. Sometimes ordained women feel they must act with greater authority and rigidity than their male counterparts to "prove" that they are really worthy ministers. Even more typically, ordained women find themselves assigned as associate pastors to a male senior minister, a situation which often quickly degenerates into the worst wife-husband dynamics. Nevertheless, however successful individual women may be in embodying their own vision of Christian ministry, the simple existence of an ordained class of women separate from lay women further divides and marginalizes any feminist influence. Clergy women tend to develop their own networks and organizations separately from lay women's groups and find participation as equals with lay women in church groups or even in support groups difficult. Between denominational divisions and clergy-laity divisions, Protestant feminists are thoroughly isolated and robbed of effective power bases.

The third characteristic of Protestantism that thwarts feminists efforts is its emphasis on the individual rather than the community. In the early years of the Puritan settlement in New England, the right to vote was based on church membership, and church membership could only be won by each individual (male) being able to give a credible account of his personal experience of grace.[6] Founded on the "inner-worldly asceticism" of the Reformation and refined by the Calvinistic doctrine of the unique worldly "calling" fashioned by God for each person,[7] a staunch individualism occupies the center of the historic Protestant experience. The critical issue for salvation is the relation of each individual to God, not participation in certain groups or performance of certain rituals, although both of these latter actions have their places. It is this stress on the state of the individual soul that has encouraged the importance of conversion and revivalism in Protestantism. Moreover, this individual emphasis tends to foster a more private or personal vision of the good rather than a public or social one.[8] Yet, for feminists it is vital to recognize the systemic nature of patriarchal oppression, rather than being totally occupied with its local and private manifestations. Asserting that none of us are liberated until all of us are liberated is not exaggerated rhetoric but the realization of the pervasive, systemic structure of oppression.

I am not saying that Protestant feminists tend to be self-centered and concerned only with their own pain, whereas non-Protestants are universalistic in their aims. It is just that the heavy value placed on the individual in Protestantism may encourage a shorter vision, focused on more immediate and limited objectives, like, for example, ordination or the election of a woman bishop, or on *ad hoc* responses to blatant instances of discrimination. Such short-term goals are obviously important, but they cannot substitute for a more broadly sustained social and systemic critique of oppression in all its various forms. African-American Protestant women have been much less distracted by this individual bias than their European-American sisters, perhaps because their double oppression, both racial and sexual, forces a broader assessment of the causes and structures of oppression in Western society and perhaps also because the social function of the Black Church in a segregated society and its roots in African tribal culture have served to mitigate the privatizing influence of Protestant individualism. Greater conversation between

African-American and European-American Protestant women might be one way of keeping the longer-range issues of oppression more clearly in view.

Since in the traditional Protestant formulation each individual was to work at her or his specific divine "calling" in the world as a holy person, separate orders of religious men and women were discouraged. The model of a women's community, allowing greater independence and communication among women than society at large generally permitted, was essentially lost to Protestant women by the Reformation.[9] Instead, woman's divine "calling" in the world as wife and mother was emphasized. Unlike Catholic women, Protestant women have had little opportunity or encouragement to define their religious identity in relation to other women or even to see that model as a possibility, for orders of Protestant nuns are rare. The religious identity of most Protestant women is defined primarily in relation to the family unit. Hence, Protestant individualism has acted also to stress Protestant familialism: the family as the focus of worship and Christian formation (as, for example, in "The family that prays together, stays together").

This familial emphasis has been so inculcated in many Protestant women that attempts to organize women-only retreats, worship services, or even meetings raises conflicting emotions in people otherwise committed to feminist issues. To exclude husbands, brothers, and sons even from those essential events required for women to raise their own level of consciousness, to learn how to support each other, or to begin to bond together to overcome generations of isolation seems to some a violation of true Christian love and discipleship. However, these actions are seen as violations mainly because for most Protestants the family has been made the ideal focus of one's religious identity. To the degree that ideas of Women-Church or the *ekklēsia* of women inevitably demand some amount of separatism, Protestant women often find them difficult to harmonize with their own tradition.

While each of these three characteristics of Protestantism has serious implications for the future of Protestant feminists, their combined weight may explain why the most important and compelling formulations of a feminist vision for contemporary Christianity have come by and large from the Catholic community.[10] I in no way mean to denigrate the important contributions of some Protestant feminist theologians and biblical scholars,[11] but any fair appraisal of the scene would have to acknowledge the wider role of women formed by the Catholic tradition. If Protestantism is to be challenged and changed by feminism or, to put it another way, if Protestant feminists are to find some means of remaining in their tradition, the many problems raised by the role of scripture, Protestant diversity, and individualism must be addressed in a serious and sustained fashion. As a first step in that broader discussion, I would like to examine the role of scripture in Protestantism and delineate possible feminist responses to it.

Sola Scriptura

Deeming it the sole authority in all matters religious, the early Protestant reformers used scripture to purge what they viewed to be a decadent and decayed Church. Scripture liberated them from the teaching of the Church Fathers and from the ecclesiastical structures which had developed over 1,500 years of Church life. Since according to Luther not even the revelations of angels could supercede scripture,[12] all authority was vested in the Word of God, including the authority to interpret itself. Thus, elaborate allegorical readings were to be rejected, and the task of minutely studying scripture in order to establish its own meanings was begun, a task upon which we are still engaged almost 500 years later.[13] For Protestants, the central and unavoidable problematic posed by the role of scripture is its *authority*, but exactly what that authority entails varies from denomination to denomination and indeed is often a hotly contested issue within denominations.[14] So, rather than beginning with theoretical debates over authority, an argument which I will eventually have to enter, I wish to begin with the simpler question of *functions:* how does scripture function in Protestantism?

Although within the diversity of Protestantism generalizations are somewhat suspect, it seems justifiable to say that most Protestant worship centers on scripture: in public ceremonies, scripture readings and sermons based on scripture (though occasionally the connection between the scripture and the sermon may be rather tenuous) form the heart of the service with other liturgical elements (prayers, music, or eucharist) sharing greater or lesser amounts of attention; in private devotionals, scripture reading and prayer are the essentials. Scripture, then, for Protestants becomes the primary medium of communion with God; if Catholics commune with God mainly through participation in the sacraments, and especially the mass, Protestants commune with God through scripture. Neill Hamilton's assessment of scripture is representative of the Protestant perspective: "God,

who is the Father of our Lord and Savior, Jesus Christ, for a certainty
spoke in these writings, and this same God continues to speak
through their witness. The New Testament is where to go to listen
for the 'call.' "[15] The crucial images have to do with "call," "speak,"
and "listen." For Protestants, the Bible is not simply a source of
knowledge about God or the early Christians or the Hebrew people;
it is, rather, a source for *experiencing, hearing,* God or God-in-Jesus in
each present moment of life.

Nevertheless, Protestant feminists along with their Roman Catholic
and Jewish sisters must also acknowledge that this same Bible is
often misogynistic and anti-Semitic, thoroughly androcentric and
patriarchal, and seeped in ancient Near Eastern and Hellenistic
mythology.[16] Indeed, along with many of the so-called "classics" of
Western literature, the Bible continues to exercise over women, and
other oppressed groups like homosexuals, a form of "textual harassment,"[17] appropriating social discrimination into textual structures
and categories. To excuse the Bible, or other "great" literature, for
these acts of textual violence on the grounds that they are simply
reflecting the social ethos of earlier cultures is either to underestimate
the continuing power of these alienating images or to approve tacitly
the existence of oppression in times past just because they are past.[18]
Jewish and Christian feminists, and especially Protestant feminists
whose religious formation has been so permeated by scripture, are
thus faced with a difficult dilemma: honesty and survival as whole
human beings requires that we point out and denounce the pervasive
patriarchal hierarchies of oppression, both social and sexual, that
populate the Bible, and yet at the same time we must also acknowledge the degree to which we have been shaped and continue to be
nourished by these same writings. How are we, then, to understand
"the same Bible as enslaver and liberator"?[19]

Feminist Responses

At present the predominant feminist scholarly response to biblical
androcentrism is to use the text, not as an authority in and of itself,
but as a source for reconstructing the history of women in early
Christianity or Judaism.[20] This approach, which understands the
Bible as prototype rather than archetype,[21] has many advantages: it
employs a well-recognized mode of analysis, the historical-critical
method, with appropriate feminist modifications;[22] it frees feminists
from the chains of extant textual formulations by judicious appeal to

the disciplined exercise of the "historical imagination"; it reveals the androcentric biases of most male reconstructions of early Christianity or Judaism by proving that the available evidence does not inevitably lead to the conclusion of women's marginality; it empowers a new vision of an egalitarian community by uncovering the leadership roles and full participation of women in the historical development of early Christianity and Judaism; and it unequivocally asserts the damaging patriarchal tone of scripture as a whole and thus allows women to reject its "textual harassment" and shift the locus of revelation from text to history and from ecclesial authority to women's community. Moreover, influenced by the Protestant principle of returning to the purer origins as a corrective for current degeneration, historical reconstructions of early Christianity or the historical Jesus have always sprung from overt, or more often covert, reforming aims.[23] Feminist reconstructions are indeed no more of an advocacy stance than other reconstructions; they are simply more honest and open about their advocacy than white, male reconstructions have tended to be.

Along with these definite advantages, the feminist response of historical reconstruction has, as does any well-defined perspective, a number of limitations. All historical reconstructions face the difficulty of establishing which point in the historical origins ranks as the purest and thus possesses the authority to stand in judgment over later degeneration. For Luther, the New Testament period as a whole held that authority,[24] but for later historical critics considerably narrower slices of that period are demonstrably purer, be they Paul's missionary activity, the historical Jesus' *ipsissima verba*, or the egalitarian movement called forth by Jesus. These contending points of historical authority are often related—not surprisingly—to the advocacy stances that generated the reconstruction in the first place and have perhaps served to return some of the flexibility of interpretation to scripture that was lost when the historical consciousness of the Enlightenment dethroned allegorical interpretation. However, if one hopes that by moving from ancient androcentric texts to historical reconstructions one has escaped patriarchal biases or reduced the polyvalent text to the objective, unitary truth of history, one is greatly mistaken: reconstructions are just as subject to advocacy and just as polysemous as any text has been.

More seriously, rooting authoritative revelation in a particular historical moment suggests that those groups not participating in that moment are somehow less worthy than those who do. Just such an assumption has undergirded the second-class status assigned to women by Christian patriarchy, for, so one argument goes, since Jesus chose twelve men as his disciples, women should not now be ordained as priests or ministers. While feminist reconstructions have done much to explode the patriarchal myth of women's marginality in early Christianity, the underlying assumption that historical participation is a necessary prerequisite for full status in the present has not really been challenged. Hence, other groups who cannot reconstruct their historical participation (as, for example, certain racial groups, homosexuals, handicapped people,[25] etc.) still face disenfranchisement. Unless male and female are seen to be the most basic categories of existence and thus, establishing the presence of both in the formative history of Judaism or Christianity empowers all people of whatever other identity groups, retaining the importance of historical participation will inevitably continue to relegate some people to marginal status.

Finally, from the perspective of Protestant feminists, reconstructions of the leadership roles of women in early Christianity, although adding vital elements to our formerly solely patriarchal picture of early Christianity, does not address the pressing question of how to work with biblical texts as they stand, considering their central function in Protestant worship and religious formation. Furthermore, in excavating the text for history, reconstructions by-pass, and consequently fail to explain, the curious dynamic experienced even by many feminists: reading admittedly androcentric, occasionally misogynous, texts can still fill women with the passion for and vision of liberation. How is it that texts that negate the experience of women and define them as "other" are also texts that women continue to wish to claim as their own—and not out of ignorance but out of the realization that they have actually experienced these "negative" texts as liberating? Raising this last point suggests another direction for a feminist response to scripture, not as a substitute for historical reconstruction but as an additional alternative to it: the exploration of gender in relation to the reading of texts.

Gender and Reading

Various analyses of what is involved in the whole process of reading have dominated the debates in literary-critical circles during the last decade as interest in so-called "audience-oriented" or "reader-response" criticism has grown.[26] Feminist literary criticism, beginning in this country in the early 1970's with Kate Millett's *Sexual*

Politics, has now entered those debates by raising the question of the relation of gender to reading. Although the "canon" of literature faced by feminist literary critics is rather more malleable than the one faced by feminist biblical critics, many of the same issues (e.g., the invisibility of women writers, misogynous characterization, and thoroughly androcentric texts) arise in both. Indeed, the stages through which feminist literary criticism has developed since the early 1970's reveal a striking correspondence to feminist biblical interpretation. Elaine Showalter suggests that three stages in the progression of feminist literary criticism can be perceived:[27] the first stage "concentrated on exposing the misogyny of literary practice"[28] both in its negative, stereotypical image of women and in its assumption of women's lesser status as writers and critics. From Elizabeth Cady Stanton's *Woman's Bible* to Mary Daly's *The Church and the Second Sex* to collections of essays on the plight of women throughout church history, like Rosemary Radford Ruether's *Religion and Sexism* to analyses of the textual violence against women in the Bible, like Phyllis Trible's *Texts of Terror,* one of the earliest and continuing tasks of feminists in religion has been to document the overwhelming misogyny of Western religious traditions.

For feminist literary criticism the second phase "was the discovery that women writers had a literature of their own, whose historical and thematic coherence, as well as artistic importance, had been obscured by . . . patriarchal values. . . ."[29] The recovery of the tradition of women as writers was and remains one of the most important contributions of feminist literary critics. This reconstruction of women's literary tradition parallels the discovery and reconstruction of women's leadership roles in the birth and development of Judaism and Christianity, the current predominant feminist response to religious patriarchy. For many literary critics, establishing the roots and tradition of female literature remains the most vital contribution feminist scholars can make to the battle against patriarchy. For others, however, although such reconstituting of the literary universe must be pursued as far as possible, the end result will still be unsatisfying because patriarchal values and institutions not only ignored the women who did write, they actually prevented many talented women from writing at all. Similarly, after every fleeting hint in scripture of the historical role of women in biblical times has been tracked down and every story involving women characters has been explicated, the sum total will still be only one coin in ten,[30] the other nine manifesting the androcentric economy. Patriarchy and misogyny are not simply textual entities; they were and are cultural, social realities that fix definite limits to the participation and power of women in every age, including our own.

Given the finite limits of historical reconstructions, a third phase of feminist literary criticism has recently begun that demands "not just the recognition of women's writing but a radical rethinking of the conceptual grounds of literary study, a revision of the accepted theoretical assumptions about reading and writing that have been based entirely on male literary experiences."[31] I am proposing the need for just such a phase of radical revisioning of the accepted assumptions concerning scriptural interpretation and authority in feminist religious circles. Feminist revision, in Adrienne Rich's words, is "the act of looking back, of seeing with fresh eyes, of entering an old text from a new critical direction."[32] One such "new critical direction" is reading the old androcentric texts of the Bible *as women*, out of the experience of being women in a patriarchal world. The texts themselves are not discarded nor are they used only as mines for a few precious glimpses of women's history; they are rather to be re-read from a new perspective, that of women reading as women. Much recent feminist literary criticism has been charting the course for this kind of revisioning by exploring the relation of gender and reading.[33]

Such revisioning begins with the insight that readers make meaning. Scripture never has—nor ever could—interpret itself. Claims of that kind have been used to mask the institutional biases of authorized interpretations. Even the history of modern biblical research reveals the degree to which various scriptural interpretations are colored by the concerns and predispositions of each interpreter.[34] While one may wish to take a moderating position that views the meaning of a text as the *interaction* of reader and text rather than simply the action of the reader,[35] it nevertheless remains obvious that readers propose the meanings of texts which other groups of readers must then evaluate for themselves. That those evaluations occasionally result in a consensus of opinion indicates a second major aspect of the reading process: readers do not make meanings *ex nihilo*. Readers in every age are controlled to some degree in the meanings they construe by the dominant conventions of reading and writing governing the period.[36]

Moreover, these conventions, usually absorbed during each person's educational and cultural development, are rarely discussed openly; they are rather the conventional "frames" orienting all other intellectual intercourse and are often referred to as one's critical "sensibility" or "taste." They guide the way writers of an age write and readers of an age read, if they wish to be judged as good writers or perceptive readers. Realism, historical consciousness, and objectivity are conventions that have shaped modern discourse in the last two centuries, although objectivity is finally beginning to fade under the attack of psychoanalytic and Marxist ideological suspicion. It is also evident that conventions shift from age to age so that what passed as reliable and intelligible discourse in one period may be rejected by another. The striking demise of allegorical interpretation since the Enlightenment is a prime example of such a shift. Yet, both the intricate four-fold allegorical method of the medieval period and the historical-critical method of the Enlightenment are conventions of reading quite foreign to the periods in which most of the biblical texts were written.[37] Consequently, while it might be possible to reconstruct some of the conventions governing the writing and reading/ hearing process of Hellenistic literature and thus gain some insight concerning how the New Testament texts, for example, might have been read/heard by their earliest audiences,[38] such a procedure has not been the major concern of religious establishments for the very good reason that the biblical texts are assumed to have contemporary rather than simply antiquarian relevance.[39] So every age has seen in the biblical texts the reflections of their own concerns, issues, and dilemmas.

The realization that readers make meanings acts to relativize all interpretations of biblical texts and should allow women to reread them as women in open challenge to the dominant androcentric or patriarchal readings of the establishment. Only, unfortunately, it is not that easy. Though many of the conventions molding the writing and reading processes of various ages have indeed altered, at least one convention has stubbornly resisted change: the view that the ideal reader and the ideal writer are always *male*. Feminist literary critics by raising the issue of gender in relation to the conventions of reading have demonstrated the dramatic power of "male as norm" on the history of Western literature and on the generations of women schooled in its image.[40] Since the male has been presented as normal and universal with the female as marginal and deviant, women have been forced to learn male language and identify—against themselves—with the male experience. As Judith Fetterley argues:

> Though one of the most persistent of literary stereotypes is the castrating bitch, the cultural reality is not the emasculation of men by women but the *immasculation* of women by men. As readers and teachers and scholars, women are taught to think as men, to identify with a male

point of view, and to accept as normal and legitimate a male system of values, one of whose central principles is misogyny.[41]

The long-term effects of the immasculation process on women, Fetterley asserts, "is self-hatred and self-doubt"; "Intellectually male, sexually female, one is in effect no one, nowhere, immasculated."[42] What is true of the Western literary tradition is even more true of the Western religious tradition. That the biblical texts are overwhelmingly androcentric forces women to identify with a male perspective (e.g. Jacob getting Leah when he wanted Rachel; David wanting Bathsheba and plotting the demise of Uriah; Jesus choosing twelve men as disciples, etc.) in order simply to follow the story-line; we must, in other words, imagine ourselves as male in order to fulfill the conventional role of reader. In the case of scripture the underlying message is that to be addressed by God, to be a full member of the divinely created universal order, we must pretend we are male and consequently pretend that we are *not female*.

Since the immasculation process begins with the earliest experiences of reading and culture, women must now consciously work to exorcise "the male mind that has been implanted in us."[43] The first step in the feminist radical re-reading of scripture is, then, to become a resisting, suspicious reader, to refuse to agree to the "male as norm" role assigned to the reader by androcentric conventions. Because the male identity has been so thoroughly embedded in our experience, accomplishing this first step will require women to help each other read together in a new way, naming the androcentric perspective each time it appears and hence freeing ourselves to see it for what it is. Such an action assumes theologically that revelation and authority do not occur *in* the Bible, nor did they occur once upon a time *in* some historical past; rather, revelation and thus authority come now in the present experience of the believer, who with others begins the task of re-visioning the past in order to live as a full human being in the present and in the future.

Can the response many feminists have had of experiencing liberation in androcentric biblical texts be explained by the immasculation process? Surely, some of it can, for by submerging our female reality and identifying with the male, we can, like Moses, lead our people to freedom or we can, like the disciples in Matthew, receive the commission to spread the gospel to the world. However, I suspect there is more to this response than immasculation alone accounts for. If androcentrism assumes male as universal, feminism in rejecting that assumption must be careful not to reject the universal as part of female experience as well. As Sandra Gilbert has pointed out, feminism and humanism should not "be mutually contradictory terms."[44] Some androcentric texts—not all—clearly do touch authentic human desires and experiences: hopes for liberation, love, companionship, integrity, justice, and peace—what Patrocinio Schweichart calls the "utopian vision." These "male texts merit a dual hermeneutic: a negative hermeneutic that discloses their complicity with patriarchal ideology, and a positive hermeneutic that recuperates the utopian moment."[45]

Thus, the second step in the feminist radical re-reading of scripture in the case of *some, not all,* biblical texts is to retrieve the genuinely liberational ideology that gives to them their basic emotional power. In order to perform this hermeneutic of recuperation, certain reading strategies may prove useful. Schweichart proposes that feminists use role reversal in reading some texts. Imagining Jesus and the twelve as women and a man anointing her head with oil (Mark 14:3–9) gives an entirely different, almost satiric, feel to Mark's story, suggesting perhaps that a heavier sexual stereotyping underlies the episode than one might suspect at first reading. Alternatively, substituting a female synagogue leader and a female prostitute for the Pharisee and tax-collector in Luke's parable (Luke 18:9–14) alters the story's emotional effect and point not at all, providing an insight into its more universal claims. Other such strategies will need to be worked out as women re-read biblical texts *as women.*

Entering biblical texts from a new critical direction founded on a conscious understanding of both the thoroughly androcentric nature of the texts and the freedom of women as readers to make their own meanings provides another option in addition to historical reconstruction for Jewish and Christian feminists, and perhaps especially for Protestant feminists, to deal with their scriptural traditions. It has the advantage of being a way to work with the texts themselves, acknowledging their patriarchal disposition but resisting their destructive marginalizing of women while at the same time attempting to retrieve the utopian or truly liberational ideology embodied in them. It is, anyway, a place to begin.

NOTES

1. Elaine Showalter, "Toward a Feminist Poetics" in E. Showalter, ed., *The New Feminist Criticism: Essays on Women, Literature, and Theory* (New York: Pantheon Books, 1985) 141.

2. See Elisabeth Schüssler Fiorenza, *In Memory of Her: A Feminist Theological Reconstruction of Christian Origins* (New York: Crossroad, 1983) 343–51; and Rosemary Radford Ruether, *Women-Church: Theology and Practice* (New York: Harper and Row, 1985).

3. Luther's address to the Diet of Worms as formulated in the Smalcald Articles, as translated and cited in W. G. Kümmel, *The New Testament: The History of the Investigation of its Problems,* trans. S. Gilmour and H. Kee (Nashville: Abingdon Press, 1972) 20.

4. On the problems with ordination, see Sara Maitland, *A Map of the New Country: Women and Christianity* (London: Routledge and Kegan Paul, 1983).

5. For example, United Methodist clergy are members of their conference and Presbyterian clergy are part of their presbytery; neither are members of the congregations they serve.

6. See the discussion of this practice and its downfall, first in the Bay Colony in 1691, and then elsewhere in New England in N. Q. Hamilton, *Recovery of the Protestant Adventure* (New York: Seabury Press, 1981) 16–23.

7. Ibid. 10–15.

8. Hamilton argues that the division between private and public understandings of the church's mission is the single most enervating controversy in Protestantism; see ibid. 1–5.

The pervasive influence and danger to North American culture generally from our passion for individualism, when what we need are communal solutions to pressing social problems, has been superbly analyzed in Robert Bellah, Richard Madsen, *et al.*, *Habits of the Heart: Individualism and Commitment in American Life* (New York: Harper & Row, 1985).

9. See the excellent discussion of the losses and gains of women in the Reformation in Jane Dempsey Douglass, "Women and the Continental Reformation" in R. Radford Ruether, ed., *Religion and Sexism: Images of Woman in the Jewish and Christian Traditions* (New York: Simon and Schuster, 1974) 292–318.

10. Mary Daly, Rosemary Radford Ruether, and Elisabeth Schüssler Fiorenza, to name but three, have contributed extensive foundational work of great diversity, clarity, and depth.

11. Certainly Sallie McFague and Letty Russell in theology and Phyllis Trible in biblical studies have provided major feminist studies.

12. "It is the Word of God that is to determine an article of faith–nothing else, not even an angel." In Luther's Diet of Worms address as cited in Kümmel 21.

13. For a discussion of the relation of the Protestant Reformation to the beginnings of biblical historical-critical scholarship, see ibid. 20–39.

14. See the recent discussion of the issue of authority in James Barr, *The Scope and Authority of the Bible* (Philadelphia: Westminster Press, 1980).

15. *Recovery of the Protestant Adventure* 3.

16. It was the Protestant need to have the New Testament continue to speak to the present coupled with the recognition of its deeply mythological

nature that influenced Rudolf Bultmann to develop his de-mythologizing program; see R. Bultmann, *Jesus Christ and Mythology* (New York: Scribners, 1958).

17. This wonderful phrase was coined by Mary Jacobus, "Is There a Woman in This Text?" *New Literary History* 14 (1982) 119.

18. For a good discussion of these issues in relation to the Western literary canon, see Lillian S. Robinson, "Treason Our Text: Feminist Challenges to the Literary Canon" in E. Showalter, ed., *The New Feminist Criticism* 105–121.

19. It was with these thoughts that I concluded an earlier article on the Bible and feminism; see "Defining the Problem: The Bible and Feminist Hermeneutics,' *Semeia* 28 (1983) 113–26.

20. The major reconstruction for early Christianity would be E. Schüssler Fiorenza, *In Memory of Her.*

21. Ibid. 33–36.

22. The use of the historical-critical method may not be totally advantageous, for feminists have yet to evaluate carefully what patriarchal assumptions may lie behind certain aspects of this method (for example, its adversarial nature, in which one proves one is right by showing everyone else to be wrong).

23. See, e.g., Joachim Jeremias's claim that recovering the words of Jesus was the only way to "invest our message with full authority" in *The Parables of Jesus* (New York: Scribner's, 1963) 9.

24. Actually Luther himself rather doubted the authority, both historical and theological, of four New Testament books (Hebrews, James, Jude, and Revelation), thus beginning a Protestant tradition of seeing a "canon within the canon;" see the discussion in Kümmel 23–26.

25. The issue of handicapped people in relation to the New Testament is difficult: people with physical and mental disabilities are numerous in New Testament stories, but their affiliation with Jesus in the gospels is always indicated by their healing. What, then, of handicapped people who are not healed, whò are still blind, deaf, and mute? What is their relation to Christianity?

26. Two excellent collections of essays covering the broad spectrum of audience-oriented criticisms are S. R. Suleiman and I. Crosman, eds., *The Reader in the Text: Essays on Audience and Interpretation* (Princeton: Princeton University Press, 1980) and J. P. Tompkins, *Reader-Response-Criticism: From Formalism to Post-Structuralism* (Baltimore: Johns Hopkins University Press, 1980).

27. The following discussion is drawn from E. Showalter, "Introduction: The Feminist Critical Revolution" in E. Showalter, ed., *The New Feminist Criticism* 5–10.

28. Ibid. 5.

29. Ibid. 6.

30. See the use of this parable in P. Trible, *God and the Rhetoric of Sexuality* (Philadelphia: Fortress Press, 1978) 200–202.

31. Showalter, "Introduction" 8.

32. Adrienne Rich, "When We Dead Awaken: Writing as Re-Vision," *College English* 34 (1972) 18.

33. The importance of gender issues for reader-response critics may be seen in the interesting discussion of J. Culler, *On Deconstruction: Theory and Criticism After Structuralism* (Ithaca: Cornell University Press, 1982) 43–64. New articles are constantly appearing in the area of gender and reading. Recent anthologies in E. A. Flynn and P. P. Schweickart, eds., *Gender and Reading: Essays on Readers, Texts, and Contexts* (Baltimore: Johns Hopkins University Press, 1986); N. K. Miller, ed., *The Poetics of Gender* (New York: Columbia University Press, 1986); and J. Spector, ed., *Gender Studies, New Directions in Feminist Criticism* (Bowling Green, OH: Bowling Green State University Popular Press, 1986).

34. See, e.g., the modern history of parable scholarship in relationship to the specific interests and backgrounds of the scholars themselves, as discussed in N. Perrin, *Jesus and the Language of the Kingdom: Symbol and Metaphor in New Testament Interpretation* (Philadelphia: Fortress Press, 1976) 89–181.

35. Among audience-oriented critics, such a position would be represented by a critic like Wolfgang Iser (see, e.g., his *The Act of Reading: A Theory of Aesthetic Response* [Baltimore: Johns Hopkins University Press, 1978]). Although such a position makes practical sense, it is *very* difficult to argue theoretically, for in Iser's case one must argue that a text is both determined and undetermined at the same time. Holding both poles together is almost impossible, so that Iser's theory tends to alternate between a text-centered perspective and a reader-centered perspective, as many of his critics have pointed out (see, e.g., Culler, *On Deconstruction*, 75–76).

36. For theoretical and practical discussions of the importance of conventions, see J. Culler, *Structuralist Poetics: Structuralism, Linguistics, and the Study of Literature* (Ithaca: Cornell University Press, 1975) 113–160; idem, *On Deconstruction* 31–83; and S. Mailloux, *Interpretive Conventions: The Reader in the Study of American Fiction* (Ithaca: Cornell University Press, 1982).

37. Actually, allegorical interpretations probably bore a closer similarity to the typical and universalistic formulations of Hellenistic literature than the particular and historical conventions of contemporary discourse.

38. For an attempt to accomplish this type of literary-historical analysis, see my *Sowing the Gospel: Mark's World in Literary-Historical Perspective* (Minneapolis: Fortress Press, 1989).

39. Some modern experiences of reading the Bible might be clarified, however, by comparison with ancient conventions. For example, I have wondered whether the difference between the dominant ancient convention of using totally reliable narrators and the dominant modern convention, fostered by the modern novel and psychological character development, of using unreliable narrators and shifting points of view might predispose modern readers of the Bible to "hear" those texts as more authoritative and infallible than other stories they read.

40. See, especially, E. Showalter, "Women and the Literary Curriculum," *College English* 32 (1971) 855–62; idem, "Towards a Feminist Poetics"; and J. Fetterley, *The Resisting Reader: A Feminist Approach to American Fiction* (Bloomington: Indiana University Press, 1978).

41. *The Resisting Reader* xx.

42. Ibid. xxi, xxii.

43. Ibid. xxii.

44. "What Do Feminist Critics Want? A Postcard from the Volcano" in E. Showalter, ed., *The New Feminist Criticism* 32.

45. P. P. Schweickart, "Reading Ourselves: Toward a Feminist Theory of Reading" in E. A. Flynn and P. P. Schweickart, eds., *Gender and Reading* 43–44.

The Pleasure of Her Text

ALICE BACH
Union Theological Seminary

> That which you are, that only can you read.
>
> Harold Bloom, *Kabbalah and Criticism*

> No sooner has a word been said, somewhere, about the pleasure of the text, than two policemen are ready to jump on you: the political policeman and the psychoanalytical policeman; futility and/or guilt, pleasure is either ideal or vain, a class notion or an illusion.
>
> Roland Barthes, *The Pleasure of the Text*

MY READING OF Abigail's story, found in 1 Samuel 25, is concerned with woman as reader of male-produced literature, and with the way the hypothesis of a female reader changes our understanding or vision of a text[1] by exploring the significance of its sexual codes.[2] Formerly, in analyzing biblical texts, it was *de rigueur* to present scholarly interpretations as objective or neutral descriptions; some critics now recognize that such a "neutral reading" is no more innocent than any other. All this time scientistic scholars have been telling it slant, reading from the male point of view. The typical reader response to female characters has held them in thrall to the dominant male figures, who are accepted as the keystone of each narrative unit. Female character is defined by male response. Often the perception of female characters as "flat" results from scholars' crushing assumption that male authors have created male characters to do the bidding of their male god. A hermeneutical version of the old-boy network.

In this paper I consider the story of Abigail as a self-contained narrative unit which achieves its dramatic effect by the skillful interweaving of dialogue and by contrasts of character.[3] By examining the sexual code, I am presenting an unabashedly subjective reading.[4] Instead of evaluating and praising Abigail as a suitable partner for David, reading the text as it has been controlled by codes of male dominance, I adopt a revisionary approach, in order to explore female influence in a male-authored work. Understanding Abigail to be the focus of her own narrative, I award her an opportunity to break free of the traditional plot of love and marriage. The text lends itself to this interpretive strategy since all the other characters, the young outcast David, Abigail's landowner husband Nabal, and the peripheral male and female servants, interact only with Abigail. No other character in the episode interacts with all the other characters. Thus, even though the story appears to be about male authority, female presence shines through.

A closer examination of the sexual codes in the text shows Abigail to be more subversive than her male authors have understood. During the time and space of her narrative, she has used her wise good-sense to control her life verbally while appearing socially dependent and compliant. The moment she encounters David, she speaks. Her determination is reflected in the series of active verbs (v 23) which rapidly move the narrative: *wattemaher, wattered, wattippol, wattishtahu.*

> She *hastened* and *got down from* the donkey
> and *fell* before David on her face and *bowed* to the ground.

The first speech is hers. Before David can articulate the anger which the reader has heard him express to his men as Abigail was riding toward him, she delivers a series of beseeching demands, orchestrated to absorb the insults her husband had spoken. Well-chosen words will wash away the villainous words spoken earlier.

> "upon me, my lord, be the guilt" v 24
> "let your maidservant speak" v 24
> "hear the words of your maidservant" v 24
> Let your maidservant arrange for the gift to be given v 27
> [loose rendering]

Calling herself "maidservant," *'amateka* or *shiphateka*, synonyms delineating a lower-class woman of no power, Abigail reflects the opposite in her actions: the text has informed us that Abigail is a wealthy woman, and now we see her in charge, comfortably issuing orders, while at the same time deflecting male anger. One suspects she has spoken equally soothing words to her husband to still his rages. There is no reply from David. The scene continues to belong to Abigail. After offering the gift of nourishment for him and his men, she profers a greater gift: spiritual nourishment in the form of the prophecy endorsing David's destiny to reign as the chosen one of God.[5] Once she is assured that David has no further violent intentions toward Nabal, she dissociates herself from this husband, who she concedes has no hope of survival (vv 25-26), and seeks to link herself with David. "When YHWH has made good his promises to my *lord*, may you remember your *maidservant*" (v 31). Throughout her speech, Abigail continues to emphasize a power hierarchy, repeatedly calling David *'adoni* and herself *'amateka/shiphateka*. While her actions show that she is accustomed to controlling situations, her words assure David that she is handing over power to him. Abigail's cloying humility is a result of her belief in her own words of prophecy. Her deference to the landless pauper underscores David's position as prince in disguise. We are in no doubt that Abigail would not herald a rogue with words suited to royalty.

Abigail's ability to act halts the negative progress of the story. The young men, who reported the foul acts of Nabal (vv 14-17), are incapable of reversing their master's action. Abigail, the woman, acts swiftly. Nabal had refused to give David *bread and wine and meat* (v 11); Abigail gathers up extravagant amounts of those items and more. "Two hundred *loaves*, two skins of *wine*, five dressed *sheep*, five seahs of parched grain, one omer of raisins, and two hundred fig cakes" are brought to David (v 18).

A central illustration of her verbal power is provided in Abigail's prophecy. Her words echo and elaborate Saul's acknowledgment (chap. 24) that David will become the next king of Israel. But her words have a more powerful effect on David than Saul's had; they stop him from committing a violent act. In the previous episode in the cave, David had spared Saul's life *before* Saul extracted David's promise of protection. Abigail's words to David change the course of his action toward Nabal, and possibly the echo of her prophecy in chap. 26 guides David's hand when he so flamboyantly seizes, then returns, Saul's spear.

One impression of the patrician landowner's wife is that she is the maternal wife of order and control. She sets limits on her husband's refusal to comply with David's request; she brings calm to David's fury. The biblical author does not consider Abigail merely as the good mother. If she were, she would have been rewarded with a long life (in the text) and a top-rated male heir, a common patriarchal convention for conferring praise on a biblical woman. For a moment Abigail steps outside the bounds of convention: a woman succeeds in stopping the future king from committing bloodguilt. But in exercising power and speaking in her own distinctive voice, perhaps Abigail has been guilty of the crime of female ambition. In order for male power to be restored, her voice must be stifled. Her recorded moment of prophecy is not to be repeated.

Scholarly readings of Abigail's story have often reduced it to "1 Samuel 25," that is, the commentators' somewhat mechanical explanation of how David annexed his second wife and the valuable territory south of Jerusalem. Perhaps that is why Abigail has no passionate admirers. Few have taken pleasure in her text.

Suppose we befriend for a moment this woman brave enough to ride out from the closed security of her home to face the storms of her husband's enemy. Instead of imprisoning her in the language of *wife*, let her break those restraints and relate to other women. We know she is strong and decisive; might she be capable of sustaining friendships, perhaps with Michal and Bathsheba? As Elizabeth Abel discovered in her study of women's friendships, "through the intimacy which is knowledge, friendship becomes a vehicle of self-definition for women, clarifying identity through relation to an other who embodies and reflects an essential aspect of the self."[6] Might Abigail comfort Bathsheba on the death of her baby? Did Michal return as "primary wife"; or had that position been claimed by Ahinoam, mother of Amnon, David's eldest son? Was Abigail's gift for pronouncing the right words at the right time necessary to keep peace among the wives of the monarch?

As the story unfolds, we can contrast Abigail's behavior with the men's actions; by holding our literary mirror at another angle, we can contrast her with the other women within the Davidic cycle. When Abigail is placed at the center of her drama, she emerges as a redeemer whose action and prophecy are necessary in assuring the future role of David, the divinely chosen monarch of Israel. Is it surprising to find that the historical code, strengthened with added muscle from the theological code, inscribes a woman in the role of God's helper? Permitting a woman to pronounce a crucial prophecy remains well within the Deuteronomistic Historian's narrative program. The prophecy is supportive, highlights the role of the deity in the selection of David as king, and "emphasizes David's success in avoiding any action that would later jeopardize the integrity of his rule."[7]

Among the thematic threads that bind together chaps. 19-28 one can identify the depiction of Saul as the seeker and David as the vulnerable one whose life is sought. Holding the thread, like Ariadne guiding the reader through the Deuteronomist's maze, is Abigail, who makes explicit the connection between the "seekers after David" and Nabal. At the center of the maze, the minotaur is Saul/Nabal. Abigail's action is "providential persuasion," part of the larger pattern within chaps. 24-26 of God's active protection of David.[8] Like Ariadne rescuing Theseus, Abigail keeps David safe from the devouring minotaur. Comparing Abigail with Ariadne is not frivolous; both women figure as a trajectory in a story about men; both women rescue/protect the questing hero and then follow him to a different land. Once in David's land, Abigail is left out of David's story. Theseus deserted Ariadne on the island of Naxos. As a figure of the process of solution Abigail/Ariadne rewards the hero (as well as the reader who makes her/his way to her) with a way out of the story. When we grasp Abigail/Ariadne's thread, we follow a different path through the labyrinth. Instead of admiring the man who entered the arena to do violence, we admire the woman who led him out alive.

Neglecting to put Abigail at the center of her drama, as a primary actor, weakens her role as God's helper. Adele Berlin does not regard Abigail's words of prophecy (vv 28-31) as crucial to the narrative, claiming the insertion is "hardly relevant to the events of the Abigail story."[9] Many scholars agree,[10] however, that the primary theological function of Abigail is to speak the word of YHWH to David. While Nabal is ignorant of David's true identity, Abigail recognizes David as the future king of Israel. Her prescience is a clear indication that Abigail is God's chosen prophet-intermediary.[11] Abigail's assurance to David that he is YHWH's intended ruler and must remain innocent to do God's will is the link between the anointing prophecy of Samuel and the dynastic prophecy of Nathan.[12] In an ironic twist, the fate about which YHWH's prophet Abigail has warned David, that of shedding innocent blood, prophesies his downfall while it connects this episode of David acquiring his good-sense wife with that future episode of David acquiring another wife (2 Sam 11:1-25). Possibly Abigail's words reveal a latent subtextual desire for connection with Bathsheba, for a community of women.

Inevitably Abigail must join Michal and Bathsheba, the other wives of David who experience moments of narrative power. A clear illustration of gender politics is found in the biblical portrayal and scholarly interpretation of David's wives. Seen through the stereotyping lens of male authority, each of these women typifies a particular aspect of *wife*; Michal is the dissatisfied daughter/wife of divided loyalties; Abigail is consistently the good-sense mother-provider, and Bathsheba, the sexual partner. There is no interdependence of the wives of David, although in their actual lives there might well have been.[13] Nor is any of the three women portrayed as a woman with depth or timbre. In the text as traditionally interpreted, as well as in their lives, the wives of David cede to male domination, and in ladylike fashion allow biblical literature to privilege male gender and to demystify their own. However, by rerouting the circuits of conventional comparisons, we can clarify and restore the identity to each woman through her relation to an other who embodies and reflects an essential aspect of the female self. We can imagine alliances based upon affiliation instead of kinship and filiation.

As the only female character in her story, Abigail's isolation is apparent. When, however, we join her story to and make it part of and a link with Michal's story (Michal is essentially erased from David's life when Abigail is inserted into it) and then link Bathsheba's story to the previous two, we see female power, or self-identity, asserting itself. We can bring the women together by altering our usual chronology of reading with a Lacanian moment of mirroring. This strategy allows the women to reflect one another as whole bodies, and deflects the bits-and-pieces views we get from glimpsing a shard of each woman in the Davidic mirror, where she appears as a distortion of the male image. Such revisioning provides the reader with a method to probe the ideological assumptions which have resulted in the polarized "good wife, bad wife" stereotypes, the popularly held view of the women within the Davidic narratives.

Abigail: The Good-sense Wife

Abigail is labeled the good-sense wife, the embodiment of *sekel* in contrast to her husband *nabal*, the fool. The connection to the book of Proverbs where the use of the word *sekel* is the most extensive in the Bible is immediate. The portrait of Abigail at first glance seems to be a narrative interpretation and expansion of the qualities attributed to the good wife of Proverbs 31, who provides food for her household, and "opens her *mouth* with wisdom, and the teaching of kindness is on her *tongue*" (v 36).

Providing us with some of the details of the life of an upperclass wife, Proverbs offers a clue to Abigail's many accomplishments. She considers a field and buys it; she perceives that her merchandise is profitable; she spins, she takes care of the poor, she makes all manner of garments and sells them. Clearly she does not eat of the bread of idleness (when would she have time!), while her husband sits in the gates of the city. Not surprisingly her children call her blessed. She is rated far more precious than jewels. Perhaps Nabal thought his good-wife Abigail was a glittering gem until the morning she told him that she had appeased the greedy son of Jesse. Discovering that his precious jewel had sided with the young brigand struck the undefended hungover Nabal in his heart with the force of a stone.

Traditional interpretations of 1 Samuel 25 have consistently focused upon Abigail's good-sense works as advantageous to the men in the story: as appeasing David in his anger, thus saving the lives of her husband's workers; preventing David from committing bloodguilt by killing her husband, and of course providing quantities of food for David and his men. The moral code reflects patriarchal values: a woman's personal payoff for virtue is connecting herself to a "better" husband, one as beautiful, pious, and pleasing to God as she is herself. The rabbinic view of Abigail expands and escalates her biblical goodness. In *b. Megillah* she is considered the most important wife of David, equal with Sarah, Rahab, and Esther, as the four most beautiful women in biblical history.[14] In the women's Paradise, Abigail supervises the women in the fifth division, her domain bordering those of the matriarchs, Sarah, Rebekah, Rachel, and Leah.[15] Josephus also emphasizes Abigail's goodness and piety, referring to her as *gynaikos d'agathēs kai sophronos*.[16] This description of Abigail is close to that of the ethical paragon par excellence, Joseph, a model of *sophrosynē*, "self-control," for both Josephus and Philo. In both stories, of course, there is the motif of sexual restraint bringing divine rescue. It is understood by the rabbis also that Abigail's moral goodness and self-control cools David's ardor, thus distinguishing her from Bathsheba. The mere sight of Bathsheba enflames David to sin, whereas encounter with Abigail cools David's fervor to kill Nabal.

Kyle McCarter's summary of the narrative unit is typical of the traditional patriarchal response to the portrayal of Abigail as necessary piece in the grander Davidic mosaic: "the partnership of such a wife bodes well for David's future, not only because of her good intelligence and counseling skills, but also because she is the widow of a very rich Calebite landowner."[17] Jon Levenson characterizes Abigail as one who "rides the crest of the providential wave into personal success."[18] His view of her as an opportunistic surfer is no more complete than McCarter's wife of mergers and land deals. The pleasure of her text comes from acknowledging both these aspects of Abigail and celebrating her subtleties and contradictions.[19]

Although the biblical author describes Abigail as *wipat to'ar*, her beauty is apparently not the sort to inspire sexual desire (*pace* to the ancient aggadists who have dreamed on paper of her) since there is no hint of a sexual relationship between Abigail and either husband. We are not told of any children from her marriage to Nabal, indeed if Abigail had had children with Nabal, they, not David, would have inherited their father's important estate. The biblical narrators/writers are not interested in Abigail's son from her marriage to David, referring to him as Chileab (2 Sam 3:3) or Daniel (1 Chron 3:1).[20] The text emphasizes Abigail's importance as the wife with the goods, the flocks and herds, detailing the quantity of every delicious item of food and drink she brings to the outcast David. His sexual hunger will be satisfied by another wife.

To illustrate the textual denial of sexuality to Abigail we might compare how the themes of sexuality, nourishment, and death are developed in another story, that of Judith, a different story to be sure, but one with striking similarities. A woman rushes from the security of home to halt the destructive action of a male. Unlike Abigail, Judith spends a long time dressing to please the male, to seduce him into helplessness. Once in the presence of Holofernes, Judith tantalizes him with possibility. She stays in a tent adjoining his for three days, offering words that are sharply double-edged, meant to fool her enemy into believing that she is preparing for a sexual banquet and that she has come to lead him to victory, when the audience understands she plans the opposite. Taking with her the same items as Abigail does, a skin of wine, barley cakes, loaves from fine flour, and dried fruit (Jdt 10:5), Judith brings the food to nourish herself, not to appease the appetite of Holofernes. Food in the book of Judith functions as a symbol of impending death; Abigail's vast amounts of the same food serve the opposite function. The gift of food comforts David and permits him to accept her words of prophecy. Abigail does not deceive David with words or with food. Judith serves tempting words and is herself the tasty dish.

Another textual silence concerns Abigail's lineage, for she is not the wife of important bloodlines. That connection with Saul's house is achieved by David's marriage to Michal. After Abigail's prophecy, assuring David that his own house is secure, v 28, the mosaic is altered, the royal connection to Saul is no longer necessary. As if to underscore his awareness of David's relentless rise to power, Saul, flailing in his own impotence against the challenger, gives Michal to Paltiel (v 44).[21] From the chronological order of wives in David's life, one can posit a setting of priorities of male ambition. First, the connection with the royal house, then the acquisition of personal wealth and the assurance of kingship, and finally a pleasurable sexual liaison.

Casting Abigail in the role of mother-woman represents a view of woman as a respite or dwelling place for man. She functions "as a kind of envelope [for man] in order to help him set limits to things."[22] In its positive aspect, as we have noted, Abigail helps David set limits to his fury. While this envelope or place sees the female body as offering a visible limit or shelter, it also views her place as dangerous: the man risks imprisonment or murder within the villainous other unless a door is left open. Thus, to protect himself from the possibility of her engulfing him, the man must distance himself from her, and place limits upon her that are the equivalent of the place without limits where he unwittingly leaves her. After acknowledging that Abigail has stilled his murderous sword, "unless you had hurried and come to meet me, truly by the dawning of day not a single man would have been left to Nabal" (v 34), he must limit her power. Serving David's unconscious will, the narrator turns down the heat of the female hero. Our last image of her is as she is riding subdued toward David's house, in the company of female servants, playing her role as traditional wife, obeying the will of her husband. How different from that passionate ride down the mountainside in the company of male servants! Shut away from the action of the story, Abigail is no longer a threat.

Mieke Bal has noticed a similar framework expressing the unconscious fear of woman in the story of Abimelech by connecting six motifs (identified by Fokkelman): death, woman, wall, battle, shame, folly. Bal interprets the linking of these images as a strong chain of warning from male to male to keep his distance, to proceed with caution. "One dies a shameful death as soon as one is so foolish as to fight woman when she is defending her wall/entrance from her mighty position as the feared other."[23] Abigail has defended her entrance with words instead of violence. By offering David all her goods, she keeps her own body secure. Ironically David does not risk imprisonment in her house, indeed does not even show curiosity about what might be within. Instead he sends messengers to her in conventional fashion to define her as *wife*, as though her moment of power and prophecy had never occurred.

As Abigail's absence in the subsequent text of the Davidic narrative proves, David is more successful than Nabal in keeping Abigail shut

up in his house, within her own limits.[24] Only when she breaks free
of the container of Nabal's house, does she become all-powerful,
simultaneously saving and threatening the men in the story. The
story is resolved when the narrator serving the male characters puts
Abigail in her place.

A feminist reading intent on restoring dimension to flattened characters must account for pieces that do not fit. Abigail the woman
resists being dismissed as a literary type, "the exemplum, the perfect
wife."[25] Nor is equating Abigail with mother-provider congruent if
we understand Mother to be the Earth Mother, the well-spring of
fertility. Abigail, the good wife of Nabal, is the mother of none. As
the wife of David, she is the mother of a son, whose name Chileab,
"like [his] father,"[26] removes him from her influence and control.
Abigail is clearly the mother-provider of transformation. She turns
the raw material provided by her destructive husband into salvific
nourishment. She is not the tender of lambs, but of dressed sheep;
she does not offer grain, but baked loaves. Model wife? She refers to
her husband as a fool (v 25), sides with his enemy, and does not even
mourn his death.

The Women

In introducing the character of David, Meir Sternberg has observed
that the biblical author provided a complete, formal, and ordered
portrait of David through "summary epithets" in the glowing report
Saul's servant makes about "the young son of Jesse, skillful in playing, able in deed, a man of war, wise in counsel, a man of good
presence, and the Lord is with him" (16:18).[27] Most biblical portraits,
unlike this one, are the product of the reader's gap-filling activity;
one collects shards of information as the narrative unfolds. Usually
the biblical text provides the reader only a partial picture of each
character. This is certainly the way in which interpreters have read
the relevant texts in the Davidic cycle in which female characters are
present. Critics consistently define women as foils for David's development. As we have noted, female characters tend to have their
identity stolen.[28] Traditional commentary has failed to fill out the
identity of Abigail, Michal, and Bathsheba, binding them by their
gender to the overpowering portrait of David. In Sternberg's schema
the entire personality of marginal characters gets telescoped into one
or two words: churl and paragon.[29] Thus, he robs the story of

elements of paradox. A reading that lingers over the collisions and
conflicts between characters adds pleasure to the text.

Assigning to each of David's wives her summary epithets provides
us with a male-produced map of each woman's place in the larger
landscape. Michal's summary epithet states that she loved David, a
fact not revealed about his other wives. Next the narrator tells us that
Saul gave Michal "as a snare for him" (18:21). The language of her
epithets is clear. Described as daughter of Saul and snare, she is to
spell death for David, although her love for him keeps her from snap-
ping the trap. Abigail, as we noted earlier, is the good-sense wife.
She is also wise and beautiful. But neither her name nor her epithets
are presented until after a description of her husband's flocks. Nabal
is mentioned first. David hears that Nabal is shearing his sheep and
sends his men to ask for the payoff. David seems unaware of or
uninterested in the beautiful wife inside the landowner's house. In
contrast is a later David, inactive, no longer a fighter or outlaw,
watching a beautiful woman in her bath. In this case Bathsheba is
mentioned before Uriah. Immediately after identifying Bathsheba as
the daughter of Eliam, the wife of Uriah, David[30] sends for this other
man's wife and lies with her. In this narrative the biblical author
develops themes of sexual power: in contrast to his earlier stories of
David's marital alliances, which are really male power struggles.

Bathsheba's epithets are the most telling of the three products of
male fantasy. For her creators, Bathsheba certainly provided pleasure
in her text. Through the eyes of the focalizer David we see beautiful
Bathsheba bathing: we observe her having sex with him. Then the
narrator takes over, revealing that she is at the beginning of her
menstrual cycle and then that she has just conceived a child. Bathsheba's first spoken words, "I am with child," could serve as her summary epithet. But the language of sexual intimacy continues. We
learn that Uriah will not have sex with her. After his death she
mourns Uriah, is brought to David's house, becomes his wife, lies
with him (again), and bears him a son. The explicit details of Bathsheba's sexual life stand in sharp contrast to the absence of any sexual
language in the story of Abigail. Thus, the biblical author exposes
private matters to paint the portrait of Bathsheba as the wife who
inspires improper desire; he uses the language of prophecy and
deference to describe Abigail, the wife of legitimacy and public
acquisitions.

Examining these summary epithets provides major clues about the
fate of each woman. The daughter of death inherits death (in a
woman figured as barrenness) from her father; she does not pass on

death to her husband. In the concluding episode about Michal (her stories are split as are her allegiances), she is scornful of David, uncovering himself before maidservants. David, Michal's husband, triumphant in his sexuality, is a sharp contrast to the dispirited figure of Saul, Michal's father, holding in his hand his spear, a symbol of male potency, and failing to kill David with his ineffectual shaft (1 Sam 19:10). As Saul's life force wilts, David's grows stronger. Deprived of David's sexual energy, Saul's household is powerless: in the first episode, Saul cannot stop David from playing his lyre until Saul hurls his spear at him; in the second Michal cannot stop David from ecstatic dancing. Since there is no sexual life between Abigail and David, Abigail enjoys no further textual life either. Only Bathsheba, the wife of sexual intimacy, participates in the ongoing story of David's reign. The length of female textual life seems to be directly connected to the extent of sexual pleasure she provides her male creators.

Another contrast among the women is the way in which David wins each of them: within the consistent framework of fragmented episodes about the women, there are full reports of how David gains these wives: Michal through violence against the Philistines; Abigail through witholding violence against Nabal; Bathsheba through violence against Uriah. While Abigail prevents David from acting against Nabal, Michal has no part in the deal struck between her father and David. She is the reward of a struggle between men doing violence to men. Bathsheba, a casualty of David's sexual imperialism, has no part in David's death-dealing plan. Only Abigail actively opposes David's violence.[31] In her story, David refrains from the impetuous act of killing the unpleasant Nabal and so gains Abigail through YHWH's will; in the episode of Bathsheba, after he has gained the power of kingship, David arranges the death of Uriah in order to assure with his own actions that he may possess Bathsheba. When Saul set the bride price of Philistine foreskins for his daughter, he hoped the violent encounter would kill his enemy David (20:21). Rather David triumphed through sexual slaughter. David himself sent his enemy Uriah into battle, again the prize being a woman. David kills the Philistines with the sword; Uriah is also killed by the sword. In Abigail's story, David and his men strap on their swords but never unsheath them in battle. It is the only one of the three stories in which sexual violence does not lead to marriage. It is also the only one of the three in which there is no allusion to sexual union, or nonunion in the case of Michal. After Nabal's death, David sends his messengers to collect Abigail, "to make her his wife" (v 42). After

Bathsheba's period of mourning for Uriah was over, "David sent and brought her to his house, and she became his wife, *and bore him a son*" (2 Sam 11:27). Saul gave Michal to David as a snare for him, but with the help of the wife who loved him, David escaped the snare and fled. And Michal was left with an empty bed, stuffed with *teraphim*, an imitation man. David escapes Michal's bed; Bathsheba is ensnared in his.

Fathers and Son

In his vigorous examination of the literary history constructed by the Deuteronomistic Historian, *Samuel and the Deuteronomist*, Robert Polzin uses a strategy of "allusive readings" to make interbiblical connections among episodes within 1 Samuel. Through his comparisons of Saul and Nabal, he makes a convincing case for Nabal's death as proleptic of Saul's. Earlier David Gunn concluded that "one of the important functions of Abigail's speech, in the context of the story as a whole, is to foreshadow Saul's death."[32] But it is Abigail herself who first made this connection explicit in telling David, "Let your enemies and those who seek to do evil to my lord be as Nabal" (v 29). Following their lead, let us test connections between foolish men.

As Polzin notes, one of the major themes of the first book of Samuel is the establishment of kingship in Israel. Read through a psychoanalytic lens, this translates into a taut chain of fathers and sons, tensions of male power. Beginning with the birth of Samuel, spiritual father to both Saul and David, and ending with the death of Saul and his sons, and the kingship or coming of age of David, 1 Samuel can be read as a record of war games of slaughter and betrayal. The cycle of doom is compressed into a question in a Margaret Atwood poem:

Aren't you tired of killing
those whose deaths have been predicted
and who are therefore dead already?[33]

But the struggle is inevitable. Until the father is vanquished, the son cannot flourish. David Jobling sees the motif of heredity as the most important aspect of continuity between the books of Judges and Samuel.[34] The sins of Eli's sons lead to the rise of Samuel as Eli's surrogate son; David, the one who can soothe Saul when the dark spirit comes upon him, becomes a surrogate son to Saul and a brother to Jonathan. Jobling understands the rise of monarchy under Saul as a move toward continuous and hereditary government. There is, however, no mention of kingship as hereditary in 1 Sam 8:4–12:25. As Jobling recognizes, the theological code supports monarchy in circumstances much like those of the judge-deliverers. The king unifies Israel and does not appear as a dynast.[35] For a dynasty is "a direct negation of divine initiative in the raising of Israel's leaders."[36]

Struggles between fathers and sons abound throughout the biblical narratives. Within the scope of this paper we can only glance at those that involve David as son. As we have noted earlier, the son of Jesse refers to himself as son to two surrogate fathers: Saul and Nabal. This self-designation underscores the liminality of David's situation. No longer the child-shepherd guarding his father's flocks in the hills of Bethlehem, not yet ready to discard the time of sonship.[37] We can contrast another son connected to David, his "brother," Jonathan, who struggles against his father, but dies alongside Saul, never to escape the role of son.

From the time David flashes his sword against the Philistines to capture the bride price for the daughter of Saul, assuring himself sonship to the king, the woman-mother is the prize for the murder of the father. Michal never quite achieves this status; she remains a transitional figure, the link between Saul and his successor. Her divided loyalties mirror the difficulties of the reader in deserting Saul and taking up emotional residence with David. Although David may be the ultimate Father's chosen son, the biblical author's ambiguous feelings toward him remind the reader that David is not always the popular choice. Abigail like Michal stands between David and a father figure. On first reading, the author's response to Nabal's wife appears to be different from his response to Saul's daughter. After all Abigail is the subject of an entire chapter in the narrative. And she is rewarded with a son, even if an "unimportant" one. David flees the daughter of Saul, and neither her husband nor the biblical authors praise her for her courage in helping David escape her father. Michal, the companion of David's liminal period, is discarded like an outgrown garment. She remains childless, a daughter until the day of her death.

However, there is a similarity between the two women David has taken from older men: he seems to lose interest in them after he has possessed them and overcome the fathers their husbands represent. They are his public wives, as he publicly wrenched power from their husbands. Bathsheba, the wife of his bed, with whom he mourns the death of his infant son, is the wife of adulthood and privacy. David's victory over Uriah was born in an act of concealment. The only benefit from that marriage was Bathsheba herself. No kingship, no land, no wealth. Of course there is a future benefit for David from Bathsheba herself. From her womb comes the son Solomon, who will rule after his father.

Mother-women are at the center of the father and son battle from the first chapter of the book of Samuel through Elkanah's question to his wife Hannah, "Am I not more to you than ten sons?" It is also possible to imagine the question posed to Abigail by the young man who has introduced himself to her husband as *bineka*, "your son." Standing as intercessor between him and the father, she answers his question with resounding affirmation. Presenting him with the goods of the father, she tells him that his house will be secure, unlike the houses of his predecessors, Saul and Nabal. And she plans to follow him into the house. Lest he be overcome with her devouring power, she calls herself *'amateka/shiphateka*, signalling that he will be the ruling father, and she will be his obedient mate. David acknowledges this transfer of power by telling Abigail that he has heard her voice and granted her petition (v 35).

Earlier in the narrative David instructs his men to ask Nabal for a payoff because they had not harmed his shepherds. In other words David wants a reward because he behaved correctly. He had not invaded the older man's territory; he requests recognition from the father: "give whatever you have [in] your hand to your son" (v 8). At the rejection of the father, David responds in anger and pain and threatens to kill him. Abigail holds up the mirror to the son David in this episode, assuring him that he is good. It is the father Nabal who is evil and who must die.

The death of Nabal marks the end of this liminal period for David begun with the death of Goliath, also felled by a stone. In the next chapter, in what is to be their final meeting, David possesses Saul's spear, the metonymic weapon of sexual power, and receives acknowledgment from the father, "Blessed be you, my son David." Not believing Saul's words. David flees the borders of Israel, but the record of Saul's pursuit of David has ended. The transitional time of David's struggle to overtake the older king, which began with his battling Goliath in Saul's name, concludes with another scene of displaced victory, the death of Nabal. During this liminal period, David has depended on women to assure him that he is better than the father. In the episode with Bathsheba, he has become the man in charge. Bathsheba's announcement, "I am with child," proclaims that David is no longer a son. No longer does he need a woman to defend him from the threatening father. No longer does he depend on the ultimate Father to do his killing for him. In this story he takes control from the Father God and proves that he can kill in his own name. And, thus, with this supreme act of disloyal sonship, he incurs the wrath of the Father, who takes the life of David's infant son.

Abigail 'Almanah

After Nabal's death, Abigail becomes a widow, *'almanah*. The word is derived from the root *'lm*, meaning dumb, without speech. From the same root comes the noun *'elem*, meaning silence.[39] In Akkadian, *lēmūn*, a cognate word, means "it is bad." In spite of her marriage to David, Abigail remains a widow, that is, she survives without speech in the text. Her name is mentioned twice to remind the reader that she lives. Although she has a son, he is Chileab, like (his) father, and thus not connected with his mother. We do not hear her wise voice again. Ironically, in spite of the textual insistence that Abigail was improperly paired with the fool, that marriage gave her the power of speech as well as the power to ride down a mountainside, emboldened by her mission to stop David from killing her husband. In spite of the implication that Abigail lived happily ever after with her Prince Charming, the vibrant, verbal Abigail seems to have functioned better as the wife of Nabal. While he lived, she demonstrated bravery. She had the power of prophecy. After his death, Abigail's voice is absorbed into David's, much as she is absorbed into his household. Once inside his house, she is no longer a threat or a redeemer to men.

Living on in the echo of her story as widow, isolated by the tradition as the good-sense wife, the Paragon, Abigail is denied political agency and her own identity. At the moment at which readers conceive of Abigail as agent, as actor, as subject, they restore dimension to her. And delight in the pleasure of her text.

NOTES

1. For our ongoing exploration of woman as reader and for providing pleasure in analyzing texts, I am grateful to J. Cheryl Exum of Boston College.

2. For a feminist literary delineation of the difference between women reading male-authored texts, and women reading books written by women ("gynocritics") see Elaine Showalter, "Feminist Criticism in the Wilderness," in *The New Feminist Criticism: Essays on Women, Literature, and Theory* (New York: Pantheon Books, 1985) 243–270.

3. Flaubert, in a letter to Louise Colet, Oct. 12, 1853, thus defined his own aspirations in attempting to write the perfect artistic novel.

4. Mieke Bal in *Murder and Difference* (Bloomington: Indiana University Press, 1988) has illustrated the effectiveness of a reading strategy that employs a combination of codes, "a transdisciplinary approach." The advantage of Bal's method is that one avoids privileging one code, allowing it the voice of authority, obscuring social realities. This paper owes much of its understanding of examining codes to Bal's perceptive work.

5. In this central scene, vv 14–35, Kyle McCarter's sensitive translation reads with Vaticanus against Alexandrinus and Venetus and against MT, eliminating the name of Nabal. Thus, the name Nabal is not spoken by either the servants, Abigail, or David, until the potentially violent situation has been resolved. The loss of his name reflects the loss of his status, as well as his importance to the story. By removing his name, McCarter has emphasized the loss of the power Nabal possessed at the beginning of the narrative. See P. Kyle McCarter, *I Samuel*, Anchor Bible 8 (AB), (New York: Doubleday, 1980).

6. Elizabeth Abel, "[E]merging Identities: The Dynamics of Female Friendship in Contemporary Fiction by Women," *Signs* 6 (1981) 413–435.

7. Robert Polzin, *Samuel and the Deuteronomist* (New York: Harper and Row, 1989) 213–215. Although Polzin does not characterize his approach as a reading of the theological-historical code active in the text, his strategy of tracing allusions and repetitions within the History results in laying bare this code.

8. Polzin 206–207.

9. Adele Berlin, "Characterization in Biblical Narrative: David's Wives," *JSOT* 23 (1982) 77. Incorporated in *Poetics and Interpretation of Biblical Narrative* (Sheffield: Almond Press, 1983) 23–43.

10. See Gunn, McCarter, Polzin.

11. Jon Levenson ["1 Samuel 25 as Literature and as History" *CBQ* 40 (1978) 20] acknowledges that Abigail is the first person to announce that David will be chosen *nagid 'al yisra'el*, "ruler over Israel" (v 30) and that her assertion that YHWH will build David a *bayit ne'eman*, "secure house" (v 28) is an "undeniable adumbration of Nathan's prophecy which utilizes identical language." Levenson, however, decides that "the narrator does not present Abigail as a prophetess [sic] in the narrower sense; she is a person who from intelligence rather than from special revelation senses the drift of history, and who endowed with the highly valued initiative and efficiency of the "ideal woman" (see Prov 31:10–31) rides the crest of the providential wave into personal success." It seems highly speculative to assume Abigail does not possess special revelation. At best Levenson's tone indicates that Abigail's intelligence is a gift secondary to prophecy.

12. Splitting the impact of Abigail's prophecy (vv 28–31) by concluding that these verses are a later Josianic addition to the earlier story of David's meeting with Abigail is another way to diminish the female role in the story. McCarter

falls victim to this approach by calling the later redaction "a vehicle for an early reference to the promise of dynasty to David" (AB 8: 402). McCarter does not mention that the Josianic historian has chosen to put the prophecy on the lips of Abigail, nor does he suppose any connection between the Josianic addition of v 1, the report of the prophet Samuel's death, and the addition of the proleptic prophecy within the chapter.

13. See Carol Gilligan, *In a Different Voice: Psychological Theory and Woman's Development* (Cambridge: Harvard University Press, 1982). Gilligan argues that women typically develop different moral languages and decision-making styles from those of men. Gilligan has concluded from her female informants that women embrace an ethic of responsibility, nurturance, and inter-dependence, which differs from the male ethic of autonomous individual entitlement.

14. There were apparently only four women of perfect beauty. In *b. Meg* 15a Sarah, Rachel, and Abigail are consistently mentioned although there is no agreement as to the fourth beauty. Vashti, Esther, Rahab, Michal, and Jael are all competitors.

15. When it comes to describing women, the rabbis seem to suffer from narrative exhaustion, since they describe Michal also as a woman of entrancing beauty, who was a model of the loving wife. *Beit HaMidrash* III, 136.

16. Josephus, *Biblical Antiquities*, Book VI, 296.

17. McCarter 402.

18. Levenson 20.

19. Adele Berlin describes the wives of David with phrases that prolong gender stereotyping: e.g., Michal as "unfeminine" for declaring her love for David, and "aggressive and physical" (apparently negative qualities) for helping him to escape through the window. Collaborating with the patri-archal agenda, Berlin describes Abigail as an exaggerated stereotype of the "model wife and modest woman." See Berlin's chapter, "Character and Characterization," *op. cit.* 23–43.

20. There is a rabbinic tradition that claims Chileab was so named because he resembled physically and in his mental powers his father David (*kil'ab* like [his] father). The name, according to Ginzburg, *Legends of the Jews*, vol. 6, p. 275, silenced any misunderstanding about David's hasty marriage to Abigail. The son is clearly the son of David because he resembles him physic-ally. For similar explanation see Targum 1 Chron 3:1. David's marriage to Abigail seems implicitly to be connected with the marriage to Bathsheba. Although both marriages were impulsive, one was born of improper sexual desire; one was proper. Abigail's good name is protected by the name of her son.

21. Although Michal is returned to David (2 Sam 3:13), their relationship is anything but harmonious. When David orders Abner to bring Michal to him, he refers to her as "Saul's daughter"; in the following verse in speaking to Ishbosheth, Saul's son, David refers to Michal as "my wife." Once again

the occasion of Michal's becoming David's wife is surrounded by male violence. Soon after she has been returned, Abner is killed by Joab.

22. See Luce Irigaray, "Sexual Difference," in *French Feminist Thought*, ed. Toril Moi (Oxford and New York: Blackwell, 1987) 118–130. Irigaray argues that "the relationship between the envelope and the things represents one of the aporia, if not the aporia, of Aristotelianism and the philosophical systems which are derived from it." She concludes that man, in fear of leaving the mother a subject-life of her own, in a dynamic subjective process, remains within a master-slave dialectic. "He is ultimately the slave of a God on whom he bestows the qualities of an absolute master. He is secretly a slave to the power of the mother woman, which he subdues or destroys."

23. Mieke Bal, *Lethal Love* (Bloomington: Indiana University Press, 1987) 33.

24. For a convincing argument of the silencing of Michal within the Davidic story, especially the metonymic function of the house as agent of silence and confinement, see J. Cheryl Exum, "Murder They Wrote," in this volume.

25. Berlin 30–31.

26. Another interpretation of Chileab is, "yes, the father is mine."

27. Meir Sternberg, *The Poetics of Biblical Narrative* (Bloomington: Indiana University Press, 1985) 326.

28. By reducing the story to slogans, Sternberg's reading does not acknowledge Abigail as the initiator of action. While there are tropes of folktale in Abigail's story—the wicked husband, the good and faithful wife—outcast David makes an odd Prince Charming. His threat of violence is not intended to rescue the fair maiden but rather to increase his own wealth. For a stimulating "caution" against reading folktale or myth without expressing its ideological bias, see Mieke Bal, "Mythe à la Lettre," in *Psychoanalytic Discourse in Literature*, ed. Shlomith Rimmon-Kenan (London: Methuen, Inc., 1987) 57–89.

29. Sternberg 325–328. Even though biblical texts reflect such formulas, I do not agree with Sternberg's conclusion that the reason for verbal shorthand is to discourage further inquiry into makeup and motivation. He sees omitted features as blanks rather than gaps to be filled in by the reader. While Nabal by his very name is to be thought of as a churl, one can fill in the gaps within the text by comparing his behavior with that of his wife.

30. The text of 2 Sam 11:3 reads *wayyomer halo' zo't bat sheba'*. The identity of the male speaker who identifies Bathsheba is not clear. It could refer to David.

31. Contra Alter, *The Art of Biblical Narrative* (New York: Basic Books, 1981) 61. Alter sees a progression of violence in each of the three "discriminated premarital episodes," e.g., Michal, Abigail, Bathsheba. Alter reads each text with David at its center, missing the critical difference in interpretation when Abigail is placed at the center of her story. Her actions stop violence; the other women are not participants in the episodes which lead to their alliances with David; they are the prizes.

32. David Gunn, *The Fate of King Saul* (Sheffield: Almond Press, 1980) 96.

33. Margaret Atwood, "Circe/Mud Poems," in *Selected Poems* (New York: Simon & Schuster, 1976) 59.

34. David Jobling, *The Sense of Biblical Narrative, II*(Sheffield: JSOT Press, 1986) 53.

35. Jobling 64.

36. Jobling 85.

37. I understand the term liminality to refer to important boundaries of the hero's life. Thus, David's rite of passage is bounded by the slingshot stone at one end and the stone-dead Nabal at the other. This liminal or transitional period ends with the marriage to Abigail, who marks the beginning of the portrait of the adult David, who soon after this "adult" marriage is anointed king of Judah.

38. Abigail is not called *'almanah* in the text, perhaps because she is already considered David's wife. From the moment David tells her to return to her house, for "I have granted your petition," the reader links Abigail with him and not with the drunken Nabal, whose life seems to drizzle out of him like the previous night's wine.

39. I am indebted to Edward L. Greenstein of the Jewish Theological Seminary of America for his etymological acumen as well as for his careful reading and valuable discussion about many of the issues and suggestions raised in this paper.

Murder They Wrote: Ideology and the Manipulation of Female Presence in Biblical Narrative

J. CHERYL EXUM
Boston College

Nobody seems to go through the agony of the victim . . .
                                        Agatha Christie

IN THIS PAPER I want to investigate two literary murders. One is a
sacrifice, which has all the appearances of a murder, except that the
victim does not protest. In the other case, the victim does protest, but
the murder does not take place in the story, but rather by means of
the story. The story is the murder weapon, so to speak. The stories
are those of Jephthah's daughter, offered by her father as a sacrifice
to the deity, and of Michal, Saul's daughter and David's wife, denied
offspring and voice in one fatal stroke, and thus killed off as a narrative presence. One victim is nameless; the other, named, but both
are identified in terms of men: one, as a daughter; the other, as "the
daughter of Saul" and "the wife of David," but never without one or
both of these epithets. They thus illustrate the familiar position of
women in biblical times, as under the authority of their fathers before
marriage and of their husbands after marriage.[1] Neither functions as
an independent agent in the sense that, for example, Deborah,
Rahab, Delilah, and Jael do. Jephthah's daughter makes no real
attempt to act autonomously, whereas Michal unflinchingly asserts
herself, with deadly consequences.

The "stories" of these two women are parts of men's stories, part
of the "larger story" that we take as *the* story. David Clines has argued

that there is no "Michal story," that focusing upon a minor character in a story results in a distorted, or at least skewed reading of the whole.[2] He is right, of course, that there is no "Michal story," nor is there a "Jephthah's daughter's story," and for feminist criticism of biblical narrative that is precisely the problem. But one can nonetheless discern the submerged strains of Michal's voice and Jephthah's daughter's voice, and the challenge for feminist criticism is to reconstruct a version of their stories from that voice. This can be done at least partially, I think, by deconstructing the dominant (male) voice, or phallogocentric ideology of the narratives.

I do not speak of these women's stories in any absolute sense, as if by deconstructing the male voice, we will be closer to the "truth" or "the real story." To suggest that there is one proper way to read the text results in an authoritarianism characteristic of phallocentric criticism—a position that feminist criticism rejects in its recognition (and celebration) of contradiction and multiplicity. A feminist reading will not be a neutral reading, "neutral" or "objective reading" usually being terms for what turn out to be androcentric readings. The relation of reading to truth involves the issue of interests, and our interests determine the questions we ask of a text.[3] In this quest after literary murderers, I am no more capable of telling the whole truth, and nothing but the truth, than the biblical narrators. Rather I shall use my interests to expose and undermine theirs, in the interest of possible truth.

For purposes of this study, I wish to set aside the question of who produced these stories, of whether or not, and to what degree, women might be considered responsible for these traditions. In my opinion, that question is secondary to the issue of gender ideology in biblical material. Feminists have long recognized that men control symbolic production. Theirs is the dominant world-view that also controls literary production, with the consequence that the female perspective will be muted, if not altogether excluded.[4] Since in patriarchal texts women are frequently made to speak and act against their own interests, an important question faces us: what patriarchal function do these narratives serve?[5] What is the motive for these murders? Pursuit of an answer to this question is one option among other possibilities for feminist analysis, and one that brings to light important facets of these two women's stories. Finally, I hope to show how the female perspective, the female voice, cannot be silenced, even by literary murder. The crime has been committed, the evidence is the text, and the female perspective provides our clue for deconstructing it.

Literary murder is, of course, different from the real thing, and both of our cases can be construed as something else, which may explain why the perpetrators have gotten away with murder for so long. In the case of Jephthah's daughter, the ritual act of sacrifice transforms murder into a socially acceptable act of execution.[6] We do not witness Michal's actual death; there is no need for its description, for by the end of 2 Samuel 6, she has ceased to play any role in the Davidic house. As we shall see, poetics and ideology conspire to remove Michal as a narrative presence. There is no similar ideological necessity to get rid of Jephthah's daughter. She is the innocent victim of her father's vow. Since by accepting her death at the hands of the father, she poses no threat to the patriarchal system, her memory is allowed to live and to be celebrated within the story. This cannot, for reasons we shall explore below, be the case with Michal.

The Case of the Dutiful Daughter

The story of Jephthah and his daughter appears in Judges 11. In return for victory over the Ammonites, Jephthah vows to sacrifice to YHWH "the one coming forth who comes forth from the doors of my house to meet me when I return in peace from the Ammonites" (11:31). His daughter is the one who meets him, and the alarming similarity in vocabulary brings out the dramatic impact: "when Jephthah came to Mizpah to his house, behold, his daughter coming forth to meet him . . ." (11:34). Jephthah's response, rending his garments as a sign of mourning, and his awkwardly expressed agony and consternation, make it clear that he had not expected his daughter to be the object of his vow.

> When he saw her he rent his garments and said, "Ah, my daughter, you have brought me very low and have become the source of my trouble. I have opened my mouth to YHWH and I cannot take it back" (11:35).

It has been frequently pointed out that rather than offering solace, the father accuses his daughter—a classic case of blaming the victim. But his words also, in my opinion, express his feeling of not being solely responsible for this awful turn of events.[7] Just as Oedipus did not intend to kill his father and marry his mother but does so only because he does not know their identity, so too Jephthah did not intend to sacrifice his daughter, but utters his vow without knowing who will be "the one coming forth." Both she and he are caught up in something beyond their control.

The very act of making the vow occurs under ambiguous circumstances. Jephthah's success in battle against Ammon and his future as chief over Gilead rest upon divine favor. His attempt to settle hostilities diplomatically meets with failure and the battle lines are drawn. The spirit of YHWH comes upon Jephthah before he makes the vow, and it is not clear whether or not he utters his vow under its influence.

> The spirit of YHWH came upon Jephthah and he crossed over Gilead and Manasseh, and he crossed Mizpah of Gilead, and from Mizpah of Gilead he crossed over to the Ammonites. And Jephthah vowed a vow to YHWH. He said, "If you will indeed give the Ammonites into my hand, then the one coming forth who comes forth from the doors of my house to meet me when I return in peace from the Ammonites shall be YHWH's and I shall offer him [generic] up as a burnt offering" (11:29-31).

Is the spirit the driving force behind all of these events, or only some of them, and if so, which ones? To complicate matters even further, the next verse tells us, "Jephthah crossed over to the Ammonites to fight with them and YHWH gave them into his hand." If not a tacit acceptance of Jephthah's terms, this statement at least implicates the deity. There is otherwise no divine action in the story and, disturbingly, no divine judgment upon Jephthah's act of human sacrifice. The imposition of the vow between the coming of the spirit of YHWH upon Jephthah and the victory renders it impossible to determine whether victory comes as the result of the spirit, or the vow, or both.

The problem lies not so much in the making of the vow as in its object. Had Jephthah vowed to build an altar to YHWH, as Jacob does in Gen 28:20-22, or to dedicate to YHWH the spoils of battle, as Israel does in Num 21:2, it is unlikely that his vow would have elicited much critical commentary. Even the vowing of a person to the deity is not unthinkable, as seen in Hannah's vow to give Samuel to YHWH all the days of his life (1 Sam 1:11). But Jephthah vows the ultimate in order to ensure success, something from his household that will cost him dearly. What is sacrificed must be precious to be meaningful (cf. David's avowal, "I will not offer burnt offerings to YHWH my God that cost me nothing," 2 Sam 24:24). Not until the last two words in the Hebrew (*weha'alitihu 'olah*, "I will offer him up as a burnt offering") do we discover that Jephthah intends a live sacrifice.[8] By holding us off until the last possible moment, the text alerts us to this unusual aspect of the vow and intimates its horror.

Yet the vow alone does not determine the tragic outcome. Tragedy is assured when Jephthah's daughter, his only child, comes out to meet him. The conjuncture of these two events, the vow and the daughter's appearance, seals two fates: she to die and have no progeny; he to have no progeny and to die.[9] Jephthah takes her life "according to his vow" (11:39). There is no last-minute intervention by the deity to save the child, no ram in the thicket. In the story Jephthah carries out the murder, and the deity is implicated.[10] And since this is a literary murder, we shall accuse the narrator of complicity in this crime.

How the young woman knows or surmises the terms of her father's vow is not stated. Her readiness to accept the inevitable is striking.

> She said to him, "My father, you have opened your mouth to YHWH; do to me according to what has gone forth from your mouth now that YHWH has granted you vindication against your enemies, the Ammonites" (11:36).

The daughter submits to the authority of the father. His word is not to be countermanded but simply postponed: she asks only for a two-month respite before the vow is carried out. After a time of lamentation in the mountains with her companions, she returns to her father, and the text states, "he did to her according to his vow which he had vowed" (11:39). We are spared the details, for we could hardly bear them (compare, for example, the piling up of details in the account of Abraham's near sacrifice of his son Isaac, where a *deus ex machina* assures a happy ending). A young woman's life is snuffed out in its prime. Yet it would be myopic to see what happens as any less Jephthah's tragedy than his daughter's, for his family line comes to an end when he is forced to take his daughter's life. To commemorate Jephthah's daughter, the women of Israel hold a yearly ritual four days each year.

The Case of the Nagging Wife

Michal's "story" must be gleaned from scattered references in 1 and 2 Samuel, where she plays a significant but minor role in the events surrounding the demise of Saul's house and David's rise to the throne. For my purposes here, I will focus on Michal's fatal confrontation with David in 2 Samuel 6, though some summary of what happens earlier will be necessary.[11] Michal is King Saul's daughter, who loves David and becomes his wife. Saul and his house have been rejected by YHWH (1 Samuel 13 and 15), and David has been secretly anointed king by Samuel (1 Samuel 16). David becomes a popular hero after his defeat of Goliath (1 Samuel 17 and 18) and Saul very early realizes the threat David poses to his kingship.

"They have ascribed to David ten thousands, and to me they have ascribed thousands; what more can he have but the kingdom?" And Saul eyed David from that day on (1 Sam 18:8–9).

When he learns that his daughter Michal loves David, Saul is pleased and uses the opportunity to dangle a desirable prize before his rival, "become the king's son-in-law." He hopes that David will be killed trying to meet the bride price of a hundred Philistine foreskins. But why should it matter to Saul that Michal loves David? What do the woman's feelings have to do with it? Saul had already tempted David with his older daughter Merab—where love is not mentioned—but he gave her to another (1 Sam 18:17-19). In fact, the reward for killing Goliath was rumored to be marriage to the king's daughter (1 Sam 17:25). Thus for the charmed third time, David has a chance at what Saul seems unwilling to let him have. From Saul's perspective, Michal's love for David may be convenient but otherwise largely gratuitous. I think it is largely gratuitous from David's perspective as well. The situation is one in which the men's political considerations are paramount, while regarding the woman, we hear only that she loves. Already the text perpetuates a familiar stereotype: men are motivated by ambition, whereas women respond on a personal level. It would be much more to Saul's advantage if David loved Michal—but that is precisely what the text leaves unsaid, suggesting that David's motives are as purely political as Saul's. Note that the text tells us "it pleased David well to be the king's son-in-law," not that it pleased him to have Michal as his wife. Saul even appears to recognize the threat Michal's love for David poses for him,

When Saul saw and knew that YHWH was with David, and that Michal Saul's daughter loved him, Saul was still more afraid of David,[12]

and rightly so, for in the next chapter, Michal defies her father by helping David escape Saul's attempt on his life (1 Sam 19:11-17).

In saving David from Saul, Michal loses him, for he leaves his house-within-Saul's-house, his advantageous position as the "king's son-in-law," never to return. He does return to meet Jonathan and to conspire with him to discover Saul's intentions (1 Samuel 20) and he hides for three days until Jonathan brings him news—but all this time, he apparently makes no effort to see Michal. David becomes a fugitive and an outlaw, futilely pursued by Saul, and he manages to gain not one, but two wives while roaming about the countryside (1 Sam 25:42-43). At this point we learn that Saul had given Michal to Palti, the son of Laish (1 Sam 25:44).[13] Saul's political motive seems clear enough, to deny David any claim to the throne through marriage. Time passes, Saul is killed in battle at Gilboa (1 Samuel 31), and David is anointed king over Judah. About Michal we hear nothing until David is offered the opportunity to become king over the northern tribes. (In the meantime David has acquired more wives and many children, 2 Sam 3:2-5.) Then he does precisely what Saul had sought to prevent; he demands the return of his wife Michal as a symbol of his claim to Saul's throne. The description of her grief-stricken husband Paltiel, who follows in tears as Michal is being taken to David, draws attention to the absence of information regarding Michal's feelings. Michal's reunion with David is not reported, a highly significant textual silence that suggests a volatile subtext.

It is little wonder, then, that when Michal has her big scene in 2 Samuel 6, it is a veritable emotional explosion.[14] In the only dialogue that ever takes place between them, Michal accuses David of blatant sexual vulgarity, and he responds with a devastating rebuke. Immediately thereafter the narrator laconically informs us, "Michal Saul's daughter had no child to the day of her death."

A review of Michal's story reveals that only twice does she appear as an agent in her own right, here and in 1 Samuel 19, where she saves David's life. Elsewhere she neither speaks nor initiates action but is rather the object of the political machinations of the two men, her father and her husband, locked in bitter rivalry over the kingship. When used as a symbol to represent their conflicting interests, Michal is referred to as both Saul's daughter and David's wife (1 Sam 18:20, 27, 28; 25:44; 2 Sam 3:13, 14). The intense nature of the Saulide-Davidic rivalry, however, the exclusiveness of each's claim to the throne, makes it impossible for Michal to belong to both houses at once. She becomes a victim of their prolonged conflict, and her two attempts to act autonomously by choosing her own allegiances result only in her own losses. In 1 Samuel 19, Michal is called "David's wife," for she allies herself with her husband over against her father. She orchestrates David's escape into freedom by letting him down through the window when Saul seeks to kill him. But she thereby, in effect, loses her husband, who does not come back for her or seek her return to him until it is politically expedient. In 2 Samuel 6, she becomes once again "Saul's daughter," for she speaks as the representative of her father's house, and by doing so, forfeits her role in the house of King David.

In 2 Samuel 6, David and "all the house of Israel" bring the ark of YHWH to Jerusalem amid great rejoicing. Michal, however, is inside, watching the fanfare through the window. From her perspective we see "King David leaping and dancing before YHWH," and for the first time since telling us Michal loved David (1 Sam 18:20), the narrator permits us access to her feelings: "she despised him in her heart" (2 Sam 6:16). That her love has turned to hatred serves as a pointed indication of her suffering at David's hands. It has been suggested that as a king's daughter, Michal finds the behavior of the present king beneath the dignity of that office. But her heated exchange with David when she goes out to confront him reveals much more. It doesn't take a psychologist to recognize that David's attire, or lack of it, is not the real issue.

> David returned to bless his house, and Michal the daughter of Saul went out meet David. She said, "How the king of Israel has honored himself today, exposing himself today in the eyes of his subjects' maidservants as one of the worthless fellows flagrantly exposes himself" (2 Sam 6:20).

That nothing less than the kingship is involved can be seen from Michal's reference to David as the "king of Israel," and from David's reply, where he first takes up the subject of kingship and only then turns to the subject of his comportment.

> David said to Michal, "Before YHWH who chose me over your father and over all his house to appoint me king-elect over the people of YHWH, over Israel – I will dance before YHWH. And I shall dishonor myself even more than this and be abased in my eyes, but by the maidservants of whom you have spoken – by them I shall be held in honor" (2 Sam 6:21-22).

Notice the pointed references to Saul's rejection – "over your father," "over all his house" – and to David's authority "over the people of YHWH," and "over Israel." David's response to Michal touches on a critical issue that the narrative has repeatedly repressed but never really resolved: David's taking the kingship from the house of Saul.

With regard to what Michal considers his shameful behavior, David promises to go even further. How will he dishonor himself? I suggest the next verse hints at an answer: by ceasing to have sexual relations with Michal, by putting aside the woman who once risked her life to save his.[15] The juxtaposition of David's rebuke and the narrator's statement that Michal had no children invites us to posit a causal connection. Significantly, however, the text carefully avoids this connection. Do we have here a case of male solidarity between the narrator and David? Or should we consider other possibilities? Since it is YHWH who opens and closes the womb (Gen 20:18; 29:31; 30:2, 22; 1 Sam 1:5, 6; Isa 66:9), perhaps the deity bears responsibility (it has been suggested that Michal's childlessness is her punishment for speaking out against YHWH's anointed). No one to my knowledge has proposed that Michal refuses to have sexual relations with David, yet it would not be out of character for her. The very ambiguity hints at the text's unease about locating the responsibility.

The rift between David and Michal is not only inevitable, given the resentment Michal must surely feel toward David, from a narrative point of view it is essential, for any possibility that Michal and David have a child, who would symbolize the uniting of the two royal houses, must be precluded. The transfer of the monarchy from Saul to David is far from smooth and requires justification.[16] To be sure, Saul has been rejected as king by YHWH and David elected, but Saul has no intention of relinquishing his kingdom without a struggle, and after Saul's death, "there was a long war between the house of Saul and the house of David" during which "David grew stronger and stronger, while the house of Saul became weaker and weaker" (2 Sam 3:1). One well-established political solution to the rift between the two houses would be their union through marriage and a child, who as a scion of both royal houses might someday reign. Theologically, however, that solution is unacceptable, for YHWH has declared that no descendant of Saul may sit upon Israel's throne (1 Sam 13:13-14). Saul's house threatens David politically and YHWH theologically. Accordingly, Saul's family is systematically eliminated. Jonathan and two of his brothers are killed in battle with their father (1 Samuel 31). Abner and Ishbosheth are treacherously murdered, and the narrator goes to great lengths to declare David's innocence (2 Samuel 3 and 4).[17] Shortly thereafter, we learn that Michal will remain childless, and the way is thus cleared for 2 Samuel 7, where YHWH promises David an eternal dynasty, a dynasty in which Saul's house will play no part.

Poetics and ideology work together to remove Michal from the narrative. The rejection of Saul's house requires that Michal have no children. But the narrative goes beyond simply reporting her childlessness; it chronicles in painful detail her humiliation and elimination. The woman provides an opportunity for narratively displacing a strategic and embarrassing problem at the political level onto the domestic level, where it offers less of a threat. The animosity between the houses of Saul and David is then symbolically resolved as a marital conflict. In it David directs toward Michal the hostility one would have expected him to show toward Saul, who sought his life, and toward Jonathan and other members of Saul's family, who to varying degrees stood in his way. Michal, for her part, becomes the spokesperson for Saul's house (she speaks as "Saul's daughter" not as "David's wife") and her rebuke of David the king functions as a protest from Saul's house against David's usurpation of royal prerogative. As we proceed to reconstruct Michal's story, we shall seek in her protest another level, one that symbolizes the victim's outcry at being (literarily) murdered.

Words as Weapons

It is no criminal coincidence that in both our stories words make potent murder weapons. Not only are the words spoken by the male characters deadly instruments of power over women, but the storyteller also uses the women's own words against them. The central role words play in extinguishing the authentic female voice underscores the appropriateness of "phallogocentric" to describe the narrative ideology. The seriousness of words and their power, especially in cases of blessings and curses, oaths, and vows, is well-documented in ancient Near Eastern literature and assumed in Judges 11. Thus Jephthah makes no attempt to modify the terms of his vow by which he is bound to sacrifice to God his only child; nor does his daughter challenge its inviolability.[18] The word kills. The vow cannot be retracted ("I have opened my mouth to YHWH and I cannot take it back," Judg 11:35), and both Jephthah and his daughter are caught up in its immutable course toward fulfillment. But if words can kill, they can also heal. The destructive power of language is counterbalanced in this tale by its sustaining capacity.[19] Jephthah's daughter asks that one thing, *haddabar hazzeh*, "this word," be done for her, that she be given two months during which to grieve in the company of her companions. After her death, the women of Israel commemorate Jephthah's daughter in a yearly ritual, understood as a linguistic act, not a silent vigil. Jephthah's daughter finds life through communal recollection, though different, to be sure, from the life she might have had through family and children, the life her father took away.

I shall return below to the subject of the women's commemoration of Jephthah's daughter and its complex effect on this story. For now let us consider Jephthah's daughter's voice. How does she speak against herself? By neither questioning the man who consigned her to death nor holding him accountable. In encouraging her father to carry out his vow, she subordinates her life to the communal good. The seriousness of the vow is upheld, the need for sacrifice is satisfied,[20] and paternal authority goes unchallenged. It might be argued that she does not protest her fate because it would be useless. The futility of protest, however, does not deter Michal, who thereby lays claim to her own voice.

Michal and David engage in a battle of words in which David has the last word because he holds the power. These are the only words he ever speaks to her, words of rebuke, and they have the effect of critically wounding their victim. Unlike Jephthah's words, however, David's do not kill. Here the narrative serves as the instrument of murder, accomplishing the deed in one blow. Depriving her of children is a symbolic way of killing Michal. Denying her a reply to David kills her off as a narrative presence. By representing her as challenging the king from a position of weakness, the narrator has Michal essentially commit verbal suicide. Notice how negative her portrayal seems at first glance. A king's daughter and a king's wife, Michal appears not as a regal figure, but rather as a jealous, bitter, and worst of all, nagging woman. She has overstepped her bounds, she dares publicly criticize the king's behavior, and we should not be surprised to see her put in her place by an angry and dismissive husband. On the surface her criticism sounds petulant and exaggerated—so what if the king makes a fool of himself? But we have seen that her words only barely cloak the real issue, the political problem that the narrator downplays by foregrounding the domestic dispute.

The Danger of Going Out

Jephthah came to Mizpah, to his house, and behold, his daughter coming out to meet him . . . (Judg 11:34).

David returned to bless his house, and Michal Saul's daughter came out to meet David . . . (2 Sam 6:20).

Both our victims meet untimely "deaths" when they leave the security of the house to meet the man who will be instrumental in their murder. The house is the woman's domain; here she is safe and can even exercise power, while outside in the larger world, men wield authority.[21] The men are the leaders, the heroes whose actions have far-reaching consequences effecting whole peoples. Jephthah has gone to battle, made a vow, and returned victorious; David has consolidated his kingdom and brought the ark to Jerusalem. The men have acted; the women respond and are caught up by forces beyond their control, though somehow apparently still under the control of the men. That is to say, both Jephthah and David could have reacted differently: Jephthah by seeking an alternative to the actual sacrifice; David by treating Michal with respect.

When Jephthah returns victorious from battle, his daughter goes out to meet him dancing and with timbrels. It may have been customary for women to celebrate military success in such a manner. In Exod 15:20 the women acclaim the victory at the sea with timbrels and dancing. In 1 Sam 18:6, after David's victory over Goliath, the women of Israel come out singing and dancing, with timbrels and musical instruments. Possibly Jephthah anticipated being met by a woman—more expendable than a man (?)—though as his response indicates, he did not expect his daughter. The tragedy set in motion by Jephthah's vow is sealed when his daughter comes out to meet him. When David and all Israel bring the ark of YHWH to Jerusalem, Michal watches from the window. Earlier she had let David down through the window, out of her domain, where he was in danger,[22] to meet his destiny in the man's world of power. Having secured his position as king, David now has no need of Michal. In 2 Samuel 6, Michal occupies the private sphere of the home, safe, but excluded. References to "all Israel," "all the people, the whole multitude of Israel, both men and women," and "all the people" underscore her isolation inside. When she goes outside to confront David in the public arena, she meets rebuke and greater exclusion—losing any role she might have had in the future of David's house.

The men return to their houses, to the domestic order preserved by women. Without the house, there is no "outside"; the men need what the house represents and what it makes possible for them, the freedom from domestic responsibilities that allows them to concentrate on affairs of state. The house is both place and lineage, shelter and posterity. When the women go outside, houses are cut off. By sacrificing his daughter, Jephthah destroys his house (thus when the Ephraimites later threaten to burn Jephthah's house down over him, the remark is grimly ironic, since his house—his lineage—has already been destroyed by fire). Michal's childlessness brings to an end another branch of Saul's house; in the end only the crippled Mephibosheth and his son Mica will survive. Yet with Michal's removal, the future of David's house is secured. With Saul's house out of the way, David receives from YHWH the promise of an eternal dynasty.[23]

Virginity and Childlessness: The Politics of Female Sexuality

She had not known a man (Judg 11:39).

Michal Saul's daughter had no child to the day of her death (2 Sam 6:23).

What is particularly striking about these statements is that both occur at the end of the story, as a kind of closure sealing the women's fates; both are stated categorically, as if they were entirely neutral observations; and both are necessary. As sacrificial victim, Jephthah's daughter must be a virgin for reasons of sacrificial purity;[24] Michal, as we have seen, cannot have children for ideological reasons. Since one lived on through one's progeny, having offspring—many offspring, especially sons—was important both to men and to women (witness, for example, Abraham's concern over his childlessness). Understandably it mattered significantly to women, since women did not have other opportunities, open to men, to leave their mark on the world.[25] That the fates of both Michal and Jephthah's daughter involve childlessness indicates the extent to which patriarchal texts identify women in terms of reproductive function. Without children, the women are somehow incomplete; they have not fulfilled their role as women. If to have no children means to die unfulfilled, it also means that the women have no one to stand up for them, no *go'el* to plead their cases. They can be eliminated without fear of reprisal.[26]

The categorical way in which Michal is denied offspring masks, as I indicated above, a narrative discomfort. Does David put Michal aside, so that she, like other of his wives later, will be shut up "until the day of [her] death [the same phrase as 6:23], living as if in widowhood" (2 Sam 20:3)? I suspect so. Regarding Jephthah's daughter, the text states, "she had not known a man." What is not an issue in patriarchal texts such as these is female sexual pleasure. Indeed, patriarchal literature, and thus the Bible in general, reflects the underlying attitude that woman's sexuality is to be feared and thus carefully regulated.[27] Patriarchy severs the relationship between eroticism and procreation. As Julia Kristeva observes, it affirms motherhood but denies the mother's *jouissance*.[28] Eroticism is not associated with the mother but rather with the whore, the woman whose sexuality is commensurate with her availability. To intensify our critique we need only to acknowledge the importance of sexual fulfillment for women. In our examples, the women are denied not just motherhood, the patriarchal mark of female fulfillment, but also the pleasure of sex, the right of passage into autonomous adulthood that opens the eyes with knowledge (cf. Genesis 2–3). Jephthah's daughter will know no sexual fulfillment; Michal will have only memory of it.

As a related point of interest, it is ironic that a women's ritual (Judg 11:39-40) serves to honor a virgin. It has been frequently suggested that the story of Jephthah's daughter is aetiological, aimed at explaining the women's ritual. There is, however, no evidence of such a ritual apart from this story. We shall explore below the androcentric interest served by the women's commemoration of Jephthah's daughter. Is this really the kind of ritual women would hold, or simply a male version of a women's ritual? We do not know. We can only speculate about what form a genuinely female ritual might take were free expression of female sexuality possible. Might it be celebration of female eroticism, of uniquely female power, the power to give birth? (Already in Genesis 2–3, in a classic illustration of womb envy, the creative power of women is appropriated by the prototypical Man who, like Zeus birthing Athena from his head, symbolically gives birth to woman with the help of the creator god [no creator goddess is involved].) Is, then, the commemoration of the *death of a virgin* an androcentric inversion of female expression?

Opportunity and Motive,
Or Whose Interests Are Being Served?

The women occupy narratives that, like father or husband, seek to subordinate, and finally control, them. Jephthah's daughter accepts her fate with alarming composure. The vow is carried out, but the unnamed young woman who leaves behind no children as a legacy is not forgotten. Her memory is kept alive by the ritual remembrance of women. Because she does not protest her fate, she offers no threat to patriarchal authority. And because she voluntarily performs a daughter's duty, her memory may be preserved.

> It became a custom in Israel that the daughters of Israel went year by year to commemorate Jephthah the Gileadite's daughter, four days each year (Judg 11:39-40).

Patriarchal ideology here coopts a women's ceremony in order to glorify the victim. The phallocentric message of the story of Jephthah's daughter is, I suggest, submit to paternal authority. You may have to sacrifice your autonomy; you may lose your life, and even your name, but your sacrifice will be remembered, indeed celebrated, for generations to come. Herein lies, I believe, the reason Jephthah's daughter's name is not preserved: because she is commemorated not for herself but *as a daughter.* If we translate the difficult *wattehi ḥoq beyisra'el* at the end of v 39 as "she became an example in Israel"[29] rather than "it became a custom in Israel," her value to the patriarchal system as a model is underscored.

Michal, in contrast, opposes the system that would have her remain inside, in her place, doubly subordinated as subject to her king and as woman to her husband. Here the message is: refusal to submit leads to rebuke and humiliation. Michal speaks out against the figure of authority—the husband/king—and is silenced. Unlike Jephthah's daughter, who participates in the patriarchal system, Michal cannot be honored because she speaks against male authority. I referred earlier to women's identification in terms of their relation to men, as daughters or wives or both. Jephthah's daughter performs her function as a daughter, and is rewarded with commemoration as a daughter by the "daughters of Israel." Michal, on the other hand, is punished by being denied her function as a mother. (She also loses her status as "David's wife"; the narrator calls her "Saul's daughter," and thus she, too, is reduced to being a daughter.) Submission is rewarded; opposition, punished. The women are sacrificed to patriarchal interests that the system remain intact and function properly.

The Speaking Subject:
Deconstructing the Dominant Narrative Voice

To expose the phallogocentric interests served by these stories is not to accuse the biblical narrators of blatant misogyny but rather of reflecting a culturally inherited and deep-rooted gender bias. Thus the present inquiry seeks to read these stories without censoring them but without being confined to them.[30] The muted female voice provides the means for deconstructing the dominant, male narrative voice. What is repressed resurfaces in another form. In her speech, Jephthah's daughter submits to the authority of the father; in hers,

Michal opposes the authority of the husband. If speech confers autonomy, we shall need to look closely at how, and to what extent, these women (re)claim their stories through speech. But first, let us consider the other women in these stories, women who do not speak but who play a key role.

The women of Israel commemorate Jephthah's daughter for four days each year. Exactly what their ritual involves is not clear. The Septuagint and the Vulgate understood the verb to mean "to lament" or "to mourn"; however, the only other occurrence of the word, in Judg 5:11, refers to recounting the victories of YHWH. This usage suggests that the women recite Jephthah's daughter's story. These women, however, do not actually speak in the narrative. They remember, and their yearly ceremony is used by the narrator to keep alive the memory of the victim (only the narrative bears witness to their witness). Jephthah and the women of Israel represent two poles: he blames his daughter, 11:35; they praise her through memorializing her. Praising the victim can, however, be as dangerous as blaming the victim. The problem lies in the victim–victimizer dichotomy, a way of structuring experience that ignores the complicity of the victim in the crime.[31] If we make Jephthah the callous victimizer and his daughter the innocent victim, we fall into a patriarchal pattern of thinking. If we allow the women's ceremonial remembrance to encourage glorification of the victim, we perpetuate the crime.[32] How do we reject the concept of honoring the victim without also sacrificing the woman? We must recognize that guilt and innocence are not clear-cut. As I indicated above, Jephthah, like his daughter, is a victim of forces beyond his control; a vow made in ambiguous circumstances and in ignorance of its outcome forces his hand. Nor is the daughter innocent; she did not resist. She speaks on behalf of the sacrificial system and patriarchal authority, absolving it of responsibility. And the women of Israel cooperate in this elevation of the willing victim to honored status.

The role of other women in the account of Michal's rejection is not to immortalize, but to isolate through contrast. Who are the "(male) servants' women servants" ('amhot 'abadav), who, according to Michal, have relished David's sexual display, and by whom David avows he will be held in honor? These women are doubly subordinated—by sex, to all of David's male subjects or servants, and by class, to the royal couple, whose mutual rebukes derive their sting from the imputation of inferior status to these women. Whether or not Michal means to include the "(primary) wives of the free

Israelites" in her reproach,[33] by implying that these women are below her dignity, she aims to disgrace the king, who turns her words around ultimately to shame the queen. A class issue intrudes to set the women over against each other and to obscure the gender issue. It has been argued that using class to divide women is one of the strategies of patriarchal ideology.

> The division of women into "respectable women," who are protected by their men, and "disreputable women," who are out in the street unprotected by men and free to sell their services, has been the basic class division for women. It has marked off the limited privileges of upperclass women against the economic and sexual oppression of lower-class women and has divided women one from the other. Historically, it has impeded cross-class alliances among women and obstructed the formation of feminist consciousness.[34]

Despite its possible anachronism, this citation is relevant to our text. Michal's privilege as a king's daughter and a king's wife isolates her from the other women in her story. By having her oppose herself to these women, the narrator leaves her to stand alone against the authority of her husband the king. Moreover, the sexually charged language Michal and David use in connection with these women and *David's* "disreputable" behavior implies, perhaps, that Michal means to represent the "(male) servants' women servants" as not respectable. That is, the narrator has Michal introduce the distinction between women in a way that makes her appear haughty and elitist, thereby sharpening the unflattering picture of her. The "(male) servants' women servants" have been "outside" and gotten an eyeful of the king. Yet the "respectable" woman will not receive society's reward, motherhood.

Michal's going out to confront David is an act of self-assertion. Such boldness on her part cannot be tolerated; the narrator lets her protest but robs her of voice at the critical moment, allowing her no reply to David and no further speech. Whereas the narrator uses Michal's protest to eliminate her, her protest can be used against the narrator to bring to light the crime, to expose the gender bias of the story. By speaking out, Michal lays claim to her own story. She cannot avoid her fate, but she can protest it. She goes to her literary death screaming, as it were. Her protest thus serves as an indictment of the phallogocentric world view represented in and reflected by the narrative.

I have said that in 2 Samuel 6, Michal is eliminated from the narrative, but this is not quite the case. She reappears in an unexpected context in 2 Sam 21:8, to contradict the narrator's earlier claim that she had no child.

> The king took the two sons of Rizpah the daughter of Aiah, whom she bore to Saul, Armoni and Mephibosheth; and the five sons of Michal, the daughter of Saul, whom she bore to Adriel the son of Barzillai the Meholathite; and he gave them into the hand of the Gibeonites, and they dismembered them on the mountain before YHWH (2 Sam 21:8–9).

The usual solution is to read "Merab" instead of "Michal," with a number of ancient manuscripts, since Michal's sister Merab was the wife of Adriel the Meholathite. But this avoids pressing the embarrassing question of how Michal's name got here in the first place. Is this a simple case of confusion of women (who are notoriously hard to tell apart): Saul's descendants are killed off, so what difference does the mother's identity make? Or is it a Freudian slip that convicts the biblical narrator, an aporia we can read as Michal's refusal to be written out of the narrative? If so, the narrative still has the last, cruel word: it gives her children only to take them away again.

In contrast to Michal, Jephthah's daughter remains within the confines of the patriarchal word. Though she does not lay claim to her story, she makes some motions toward self-assertion. The two parts of her speech pull in different directions. In the first part, she surrenders volition. In the second, within the boundaries set by her father's vow, boundaries she accepts, she attempts to define herself, to lay some claim to her own voice: she asks for a period of two months in which to grieve, accompanied by her female companions.

> She said to him,
> "My father, you have opened your mouth to YHWH,
> do to me according to what has gone forth from your mouth,
> now that YHWH has vindicated you against your enemies
> the Ammonites."
> And she said to her father,
> "Let this thing be done for me,
> let me alone two months
> that I may go and wander upon the hills
> and bewail my virginity,
> I *and my companions*."

Mieke Bal wants to posit a connection between the phrase which she translates, "to lament in confrontation with my nubility," and a rite of passage, "a phase of transition that prepared her for marriage."[35] She finds here the woman's own point of view in contrast to the narrator's androcentric perspective, "she had not known a man," and she then proceeds to deconstruct the male concept of virginity via a detour into Freudian theory. Her resultant (re)reading of the entire story, a counter-reading, challenges the more traditional interpretations found within biblical scholarship and illustrates one way to reinscribe a female perspective. Another possibility of reading a different meaning into the phrase, "bewail my virginity," presents itself if we suppose the young woman's familiarity with the sacrificial system (i.e., her better knowledge than ours about human sacrifice in the ancient Near East).[36] She laments not just unfulfillment but the clear and brutal fact of imminent death, recognizing that if she were not a virgin daughter, her father could not sacrifice her.[37] Such an argument, informed by anthropology and Girardian theory, involves the same kind of retrospective reasoning as the rabbinic objection — what if the "one coming forth" had been a camel, a donkey, or a dog (*Bereshit Rabbah* 60:3; *Wayyiqra Rabbah* 37:4) — based on purity laws. I have already suggested that narrative necessity determines the outcome. The daughter's tragedy is that she — not another — is the one to come forth to meet Jephthah, and that she is an (I would even say, the) acceptable sacrificial victim. This takes us back to my earlier remarks about the coincidence between the terms of the vow and the daughter's appearance, a conjunction of events apparently beyond human control.

The most interesting feature of the daughter's ceremonial lamentation is her inclusion of other women in the event. Only at the conclusion of her speech does she reveal that, unlike her father, she has companions with whom to share her distress. *Ra'yotay*, "my companions," is her last spoken word in the narrative; *'abi*, "my father," was her first. Symbolically, through speech, she journeys from the domain of the father who will quench her life to that of the female companions who will preserve her memory.

Ultimately the text denies autonomy to Jephthah's daughter and confines her voice within patriarchal limits, using it to affirm patriarchal authority. Yet her voice transports her to a point of solidarity with her female friends and with other daughters, the "daughters of Israel," who refuse to forget (compare Michal's isolation). The resultant image is too powerful to be fully controlled by androcentric interests. The (androcentric) text segregates women: the daughter spends two months with female companions, away from her father and the company of men; the ritual of remembrance is conducted by women alone.[38] But as Gerda Lerner points out, when women are segregated ("which always has subordination as its purpose"), they transform such patriarchal restraint into complementarity and redefine it.[39] We can choose to read this story differently, to expose its valorization of submission and glorification of the victim as serving phallocentric interests, and to redefine its images of female solidarity in an act of feminist symbol-making.

By exposing the phallogocentric bias in the stories of Jephthah's daughter and of Michal, I have sought to hear the women's voices differently, and by doing so to give the victims of literary murder a voice that identifies and protests the crimes against them and that claims for them a measure of that autonomy denied them by the larger story.

NOTES

1. For a helpful discussion, see Phyllis Bird, "Images of Women in the Old Testament," in *Religion and Sexism* ed. R. R. Ruether (New York: Simon & Schuster, 1974) 41–88.

2. "The Story of Michal, Wife of David, in Its Sequential Unfolding," paper read at the 1988 Annual Meeting of the Society of Biblical Literature.

3. Mieke Bal, "How Does an Author Become the Author of a Crime," paper read at the 1988 Annual Meeting of the Society of Biblical Literature.

4. See Gerda Lerner, *The Creation of Patriarchy* (New York: Oxford University Press, 1986) 5–6, 199–211, 231–233 *et passim.* The challenge for feminist analysis is to find women's (sub)texts within these phallocentric texts; cf. the important work of Mieke Bal, *Death and Dissymmetry: The Politics of Coherence in the Book of Judges* (Chicago: University of Chicago Press, 1988).

5. *Pace* Carol Meyers, *Discovering Eve: Ancient Israelite Women in Context* (New York: Oxford University Press, 1988) 24–26, I am not willing to forgo the use of the term "patriarchal" to describe the male gender bias of narrative; this usage is widespread in feminist literature.

6. This is not to say that we are to condone Jephthah's sacrifice of his daughter, but only that human sacrifice was practiced. No outright condemnation of Jepthah's sacrifice appears in the text, but I think hints of disapproval appear in the disastrous episode with the Ephraimites that follows the sacrifice; see my "The Tragic Vision and Biblical Narrative: The Case of Jephthah," in *Signs and Wonders: Biblical Texts in Literary Focus,* ed. J. C. Exum (Decatur, GA: Scholars Press, 1989) 71–72.

7. See Exum 67–69.

8. On the debate whether Jephthah intended a human or animal sacrifice, see David Marcus, *Jephthah and His Vow* (Lubbock, TX: Texas Tech Press, 1986) 13–18; cf. Exum 67.

9. His death is reported in Judg 12:7.

10. There are many parallels where a parent promises to a supernatural figure what turns out to be his or her own child; see Marcus 40–43; Exum 68 n. 5.

11. For a detailed discussion of Michal's fate, see my forthcoming study, *Arrows of the Almighty: Tragic Dimensions of Biblical Narrative.*

12. I prefer to follow the Hebrew here; instead of becoming a snare to David, Michal's love becomes a snare to Saul.

13. Reading the verb tense as past perfect.

14. See the perceptive analysis of Robert Alter, *The Art of Biblical Narrative* (New York: Basic Books, 1981) 123–125.

15. That Michal's life might have been in danger had Saul discovered her role in David's escape (1 Samuel 19) is suggested by Saul's response of throwing a javelin at his son Jonathan, when Jonathan takes David's part (1 Sam 20:33).

16. Jonathan plays a major role in effecting the transition; see David Jobling, *The Sense of Biblical Narrative,* vol. 1 (Sheffield: JSOT, 1978) 4–25.

17. The so-called "History of David's Rise" has been seen as an apology for David; see P. Kyle McCarter, Jr., "The Apology of David," *JBL* 99 (1980) 489–504; *I Samuel,* AB 8 (Garden City, NY: Doubleday, 1980) 27–30.

18. The present story assumes the inviolability of Jephthah's vow, whereas Lev 27:1–8 stipulates monetary payment by which a person vowed to God could be released. In the midrashic literature, one finds various attempts to explain Jephthah's ignorance of the law in this case; see Marcus 46–47.

19. For fuller discussion of this theme, see *Arrows of the Almighty,* chap. 3.

20. See René Girard, *Violence and the Sacred* (Baltimore: Johns Hopkins University Press, 1977).

21. Proverbs 31 offers a good example. The woman has considerable power over the household, while her husband "sits among the elders of the land" (v. 23). The distinction between power and authority is helpful; authority is legitimate power, power recognized by society. See Michelle Zimbalist Rosaldo, "Women, Culture, and Society: A Theoretical Overview," 21–22; and Louise Lamphere, "Strategies, Cooperation, and Conflict among Women in Domestic Groups," 99; both in M. Z. Rosaldo and L. Lamphere, eds., *Women, Culture, and Society* (Stanford: Stanford University Press, 1974). See also Jo Ann Hackett, "In the Days of Jael: Reclaiming the History of Women in Ancient Israel," in *Immaculate and Powerful: The Female in Sacred Image and Social Reality,* eds. C. W. Atkinson, C. H. Buchanan, M. R. Miles (Boston: Beacon Press, 1985) 17–22; Meyers 40–44.

22. In *Arrows of the Almighty,* I explore the sexual symbolism in 1 Samuel 19, where Michal figuratively births David into freedom.

23. For very different, but fascinating analyses of the complexity of the symbolism of the house in this material, see Bal 169–196; Joel Rosenberg, *King and Kin: Political Allegory in the Hebrew Bible* (Bloomington: Indiana University Press, 1986) 113–123.

24. The situation of the sacrificial victim is somewhat more complex, but need not detain us. Married women are not good candidates for sacrifice because a married woman has ties both to her parents' and her husband's

families, either of which might consider her sacrifice an act of murder and thus take vengeance; see Girard 12–13. On the opposition between sacrificial purity and the pollution of childbirth, see Nancy Jay, "Sacrifice as Remedy for Having Been Born of Woman," in *Immaculate and Powerful: The Female in Sacred Image and Social Reality*, eds. C. W. Atkinson, C. H. Buchanan, and M. R. Miles (Boston: Beacon Press) 283–309. Girard argues that anyone who does not have a champion makes an appropriate sacrifice.

25. Deborah is an important exception who proves the rule.

26. This is crucial according to Girard 13.

27. In *The Creation of Patriarchy*, Lerner traces male control of female sexuality from its locus within the patriarchal family to regulation by the state. On woman's sexuality "not so much as part of her feminine being but, rather, as an exclusive form of male experience," see Nehama Aschkenasy, *Eve's Journey* (Philadelphia: University of Pennsylvania Press, 1986) esp. 123–124. Within the Bible, the Song of Songs is the great exception.

28. *About Chinese Women*, tr. Anita Barrows (New York: Marion Boyars, 1986) 26. On patriarchy's division of eroticism and procreativity, see Lerner, esp. chap. 7.

29. Marcus 34.

30. I adopt this concept from Julia Kristeva, *Desire in Language: A Semiotic Approach to Literature and Art*, ed. L. S. Roudiez, tr. T. Gora, A. Jardine, and L. S. Roudiez (New York: Columbia University Press, 1980) xi.

31. Cf. Lerner's remarks on the complicity of women in patriarchy 5–6; 233–235.

32. Thus a reading such as Phyllis Trible's, that makes Jephthah all-bad, irredeemably guilty, and wholly responsible for the crime of murder, and his daughter helpless and totally innocent, simply reinforces the victim-victimizer dichotomy; see *Texts of Terror* (Philadelphia: Fortress Press, 1984) 93–109. Bal, in contrast, completely reinterprets the daughter's death and the meaning of the women's remembrance; see 45–68, 96–113, 119–122, 161–168 *et passim*.

33. The phrase, "Hauptfrauen der freien Israeliten," is Frank Crüsemann's ("Zwei alttestamentliche Witze: I Sam 21:11–15 und II Sam 6:16. 20–23 als Beispiele einer biblischen Gattung," *ZAW* 92 [1980] 226), who thinks the remark refers only to lower class women. Cf. McCarter, *II Samuel* 187, who believes Michal refers to "all the young women of Israel, whether slave or free."

34. Lerner 139. See esp. chap. 6 for a fuller argument.

35. Bal 49. Her argument appears mainly in chaps. 2, 4, and 5.

36. For discussion of this topic, see Alberto R. W. Green, *The Role of Human Sacrifice in the Ancient Near East* (Missoula, MT: Scholars Press, 1975) 199. Green observes, "During the formative period of the Federation of Israel, there is the strong implication that human sacrifice was practiced by the people as an acceptable aspect of their Yahwistic belief."

37. I thank my colleague Ellen Ross for suggesting this idea. As my discussion above indicates, if Jephthah's daughter were married, her husband, not her father, would have power over her. If she had borne children, she would not be sacrificially pure; see Jay.

38. The Israelite women engage in ritual whereas the men are busy fighting, in the war with Ammon (10:17–11:33) and among themselves (12:1–6).

39. Lerner 242.

A Heifer from Thy Stable:
On Goddesses and the Status of Women
in the Ancient Near East

CAROLE R. FONTAINE
Andover Newton Theological School

THE QUESTION OF how women relate to religious systems of signifi-
cation is always a complex one. This is particularly true when we
try to probe ancient texts concerning the relationship between the
status of women and the presence of goddesses in a given culture.
The standard feminist critique of history and its interpreters holds for
any investigation of these issues in ancient Near Eastern societies:
"history," as it has come down to us through cuneiform and hiero-
glyphic sources, is very much the province of the "winners"—elite
males whose ideological interests were served by the "disappearing"
of the voices of women and other subject peoples. Added to this
inherent bias within the texts themselves is the problem of piecemeal
survival, with some texts surviving the destructions of war or aban-
donment of sites and others perishing. Nor do all texts survive in
good condition: clay tablets break or become worn down around the
edges and outer sheets of papyrus rolls may be victims of decay and
rough handling by graverobbers or inept restorers. Further, even
where text critical work is able to establish a readable text, translation
problems exist. Not all lexical items or contextual allusions are readily
intelligible to translators, and considerable debate may ensue. In
short, we do not have a complete record of past, even though biased,
sources on which to base our studies and what we do have to work
with is often shrouded in ambiguity or limited in scope and value.

The situation is even more difficult should we try to trace the development of the "historical" goddess cults from their supposed Neolithic precursors. In the absence of texts from the Neolithic era, we are forced to rely on iconographic representations, and recovery of material culture through archaeological excavation. Archaeological reconstructions of culture are no more free from the biases and preconceptions of their excavators than literary readings of ancient texts are free from the values imposed on them by their modern critics. Hence, we may observe widely divergent interpretations of a single artifact: do Paleolithic and Neolithic "Venus" figurines represent a celebration of the sacrality of the female body with its life-creating and sustaining abilities, or do we have instead male art which finds its outlet in the creation of female "sex objects"? Both interpretations appear in the literature, and in the absence of epigraphic confirmation of either hypothesis, the anepigraphic evidence retains a mystery as it gestures toward a functional meaning we may imagine but cannot "prove." We may choose to endorse Mellaart's conclusions from the evidence of burial practices, grave goods, and iconography at Çatal Hüyük that women were held in high esteem, holding religious offices and participating in the vital activities of the community.[1] We may even relate this alleged high status for women to the overwhelming presence of goddesses in the community's cultic installations, but without corroborating texts and a thorough excavation of the site, as feminist historians we still find ourselves operating in the realm of scholarly conjecture. Excavations from Minoan Crete, covering a time period which ranges from the middle of the Early Bronze Age into the Late Bronze Age, are often used to support the presence of peace-loving matriarchies in the ancient world. Here we find another case in point where speculation sometimes outstrips solid reconstruction. Where evidence is embarrassing or contradictory to the matriarchal hypothesis, it is ignored or redated to reflect the warlike practices of the later Mycenaean invaders, thereby preserving the desired view of the Minoans.[2] What we *may* say about the Neolithic Anatolian and later Minoan communities mentioned here is that they appear to be *relatively* peaceful, compared to the later imperialistic, clearly patriarchal empires of the Nile Valley and the Fertile Crescent, and that this cultural configuration was enabled both by their geographical locations and socioeconomic adaptations to their ecosystems. Within this cultural matrix, it appears that the relations between the sexes may have been organized along more egalitarian lines, at least judging from iconography and burial practices, and that the presence of goddesses in these cultures may have served to both symbolize and legitimize the position of women.

No matriarchies can be proven to exist in the absence of genealogical texts, and we must pose the question of whether or not that is something to be mourned. Feminist critique of power relations suggests that a simple reversal of the roles of oppressed and oppressing groups is not enough, at least from an evolutionary perspective (even though such reversal must certainly appear advantageous to those in the oppressed group). What is needed is a thorough-going dismantling of the structures by which any group is able and allowed to oppress another. Matriarchal rule is not necessarily the answer, so that the failure to uncover such "ideal" cultures need not deter us from the task of envisioning an alternative future to patriarchal destruction of the earth.

Once we move into the historical periods of the Bronze and Iron Ages, the goddess cults known to us are well integrated into the patriarchal ideology of their cultures. Isis, the Egyptian redeemer, acts on behalf of Osiris her husband and Horus her son rather than for herself. The Hattic goddesses of pre-Hittite Anatolia are incorporated into the Hittite pantheon, and engage in activities which benefit the new imperial power structure. The Sumerian Inanna acts on behalf of her city Uruk (biblical Erech), and by the time she is identified with the semitic Ištar, her divine power has been fully harnessed to support kingship.[3] While it is tempting to see this "domestication" of the ancient Near Eastern goddesses as an analog for the slow but steady decline of the status of women known to us from legal and economic texts, we are brought to another critical question in our attempts at reconstruction of women's past: what is the relationship of a text to the society that spawned it? Dare we assume a simple, one-to-one correspondence between literary symbol and social reality? Can a patriarchal text speak truth about the reality of women's lives?[4] This, of course, is not a question confined only to feminist discourse on history and literature, but one that consistently plagues all the disciplines.[5]

It might be helpful to propose here a model for sorting through the various types of texts preserved, with an emphasis on the amount of social verisimilitude likely to be preserved in them. The figure below represents a kind of sliding scale ranging from texts which are most likely to contain the highest degree of verisimilitude to those judged least likely to reflect social reality, at least in any direct way. It is important to remember that the creation of a text, even a humdrum economic or legal text, is still an imaginative, creative act undertaken by someone with the leisure or mandate to engage in such activities. Texts both *respond* to social reality and help to shape it.[6] Texts may be classed along a continuum of those which are based in purely referential discourse (high degree of verisimilitude) to those which are highly symbolic and expressive (small degree of verisimilitude), i.e., those which are mapped on the combinative, syntagmatic axis of language as opposed to those whose nature is more related to the associative, paradigmatic axis.[7] Further, anyone with experience of modern legal or economic texts knows that even such supposedly "neutral" texts as these may contain a large measure of wishful thinking or outright disinformation. The walls of Karnak give adequate testimony to the fact that ancient writers were no more adverse to casting recorded reality into their desired image than are modern lawyers and businesspeople.[8] Additionally complicating the task of judging a text's relation to society, types of texts may blend across genres, mixing elements that are referential and imaginative ("secular" love poetry developed from models of ritual performance of a "sacred marriage," for example, or imaginative tales which become embedded in annalistic or etiological narratives). Hence, the following model should be taken as a guide only. Texts must be evaluated for verisimilitude on an individual basis, in conjuction with study of material culture, parallel texts and comparative ethnography.[9]

economic texts	High Degree of Verisimilitude
legal texts	
correspondence (including prophecy)	
wisdom literature	
ritual performance texts (liturgies, magical and omen texts)	
prayer texts	
annalistic prose	
etiological narrative (saga, legend, genealogy)	
"secular" love poetry	
tales (*Märchen*)	
mythological texts	Low Degree of Verisimilitude

Fig. 1: Degree of verisimilitude in ancient Near Eastern texts, organized by genre

Even were we to solve the riddle of text-and-society, our problems in the use of ancient Near Eastern texts are still legion. Androcentric language was often used inclusively, so that we may not automatically assume the absence of women even when they are not explicitly mentioned as present. Further, as noted above, these texts reflect the agendas of their elite male authors and tend to focus on the public domain where male power is located and exercised. The private domain of the extended family, even though it functioned as the primary unit of economic production in antiquity,[10] is usually known to us only through hints or textual "asides" because it was not of particular interest to the authors. Since the private domain was the arena in which the lives of most women were lived out, we are generally left with a nebulous picture of women's everyday lives. Reflecting the class issues involved in the creation of "literary" and referential texts for the ruling classes, it is also the case that we know less about the lives of women of middle or lower class than we do about elite women. Generally, then, we have very little access to what women themselves actually thought about their lot in life and scholarly models of reconstruction which are insensitive to the web of considerations involved in the formation and interpretation of these texts often do not advance our knowledge.

Models of the Past

In our search for answers, we must begin by posing the proper questions. In any consideration of the "status" of women, the researcher must be aware of the comprehensive difficulties involved in such a project. As Martin K. Whyte points out in *The Status of Women in Preindustrial Societies*, there is no such thing as *the* status of women, for there is wide variability both cross-culturally and within cultures, where women's "class" identity, with all its possible benefits and detriments, is linked to the class of their men.[11] Elite women may have a quite different status than do their out-group sisters. In his sample of 93 preindustrial cultures, covering a time period from 1750 BCE to 1800 CE, Whyte investigated the status of women through use of the following variables: property control, kin power, value of life, value of labor, domestic authority, ritualized female solidarity, control of sexuality, ritualized fear of women, joint participation with men, and informal influence. Despite the difficulties in use of the cross-cultural method (inability to deal with evolutionary change in the status of women in a given culture, inability to handle class variations in status in a sample, need to rely on data gathered in ways that reflected gender-bias in either informant or fieldworker, focus on formal rather than informal aspects of the status of women, etc.), significant hypotheses were tested and important findings made.[12] Whyte concluded that no one key factor could be used to predict the status of women for a particular culture, nor was there any one factor which, if improved, resulted in raising the entire status of women. In matrilineal and matrilocal societies, women enjoyed modest benefits in status in the area of property rights, female solidarity, kin power, sexual restrictions and value of life. Male hunting, male bonding and male strength did not account for the low status of women, but cultures which were dominated by the "classical" religions (Judaism, Christianity, Islam, Hinduism, and Buddhism) consistently displayed lower statuses for their women. This last finding may be related to the fact that these religions tend to appear in more culturally complex societies (in which women generally fare worse) rather than in simpler, less stratified, and diversified cultures.[13] Whyte's study did not offer any specific correlation on the relation of the presence of goddesses to women's status, and lack of explicit focus on the religious ideologies used to legitimate low or high status for women limits its usefulness for our purposes here. Nevertheless, this study alerts us to the incredible complexity involved in any investigation of the status of women.

Low Female Status				High Female Status
Female Material Control: females create, act, allocate, dispose of land/ produce/ crafts beyond the domestic unit	*Demand for female produce:* recognized value internally or external- ly beyond the domes- tic unit	*Female political participation:* regular, official participation; influence policy beyond the domestic unit	*Female solidarity groups:* for political or economic inter- ests, females group in regu- lar way to protect or rep- resent inter- ests; are recog- nized and ef- fective in doing so	

Fig. 2: Peggy R. Sanday's analysis of female status in the public
     domain (192-93)

Specific attention to the variations in women's status when goddesses are present in a culture is found in Peggy R. Sanday's seminal study, "Female Status in the Public Domain."[14] Four variables are used to chart female power (the ability to act effectively) and authority (recognized and legitimized power) in a sample of twelve cultures:

female material control, demand for female produce, female political participation, and female solidarity groups (see Fig. 2). It was found that where women contributed approximately 40 percent to the groups's subsistence needs, their status generally improved, especially where they retained control over the allocation of their products.[15] Where systems of religion and/or magic held a favorable view of female power, Sanday determined this to be a *response* to changes in production, rather than a cause. While there was no correlation between the number of female deities in a culture and women's status, there was a strong correlation between the percentage of goddesses and women's contribution to group subsistence needs. There were low but positive correlations between goddesses with general powers (i.e., power over both females and males) and female status.[16]

Sanday's results are intriguing for the questions raised with respect to the ancient Near East, but as she acknowledges, more work needs to be done in this area before we can propose hard and fast conclusions. Further, there are elements in Sanday's shaping of the study which deserve attention. By focusing on female status in the *public* domain, the entire sphere of women's role and status within the domestic unit is pushed aside. If one of the goals of feminist research in this area is to reclaim and re-value the worlds in which women actually live, the public domain cannot become our exclusive locus of inquiry. Similarly, by attending primarily to goddesses with "general powers" and excluding those with power exclusively over women, we see a subtle modern bias at work to devalue the role of fertility in women's lives and self-understanding. While it is true that a "full-service" goddess might be more appealing to modern people seeking to expand their horizons of divinity, the "fertility" goddesses of antiquity cannot be so easily dismissed without losing important insights into ancient women's concerns and religious sensibilities. Although it has rightly been pointed out that the designation "fertility goddess" is an appellation which has allowed predominantly male scholars to dismiss and discount the role of goddesses in ancient religions,[17] it is still the case that the roles of these goddesses in promoting and sustaining fertility were significant aspects of their personalities and functions. At this point, it becomes important to remain aware of how modern trends in rethinking the "biological destiny" of women may be skewing our vision of the past.

In *Die Göttin und ihr Heros: die matriarchalen Religionen in Mythos, Märchen und Dichtung* (München: Frauenoffensive, 1980), feminist philosopher and aesthetician Heide Göttner-Abendroth uses world mythology in an attempt to reconstruct the "matriarchal mythology" of early civilizations. She outlines three stages in the development of matriarchal religions, which she understands as "religions of rebirth" rather than simply as "fertility religions" (see Fig. 3).

I. Pre-Indo-European (Matriarchal periods)
  a. early rural matriarchies: chthonic goddesses
  b. developed urban matriarchies: astral goddesses
  c. continued urban matriarchies: cyclic battle with nature demons
II. Indo-European transformations (imposition of patriarchy)
  a. sex change: Great Mother becomes All-Knowing Father
  b. role change: Goddess as God's "Wife"
  c. generational change: Goddess as Father's "Daughter"
  d. myths of rebellion against Father
  e. matriarchal cults survive in secret opposition
III. Patriarchal Major Religions (absolute father-god)
  a. abstract mythology
  b. philosophical abstractions

Fig. 3: Heide Göttner-Abendroth's stages of transformation in matriarchal religions (adapted from *Die Göttin und ihr Heros*, 119-20)

While Göttner-Abendroth has performed a valuable service in calling our attention to patterns which seem to extend across time and region in mythological texts, there are a number of problems with her reconstruction. Even discounting a too-easy identification of matrilineal and matrilocal cultures as matriarchal ones and her reliance on the scholarship of Bachofen and Graves, her simplistic assumptions of the way in which mythology reflects out-group history must give pause to historians and literary critics alike. As is typical of most attempts to develop a comprehensive, universal scheme, she is obliged to "tinker" with the evidence from certain cultures which does not fit her patterns and this results in violation of some of the basic rules of good ethnography. A case in point is her phase I.c. of developed urban matriarchies, where she sees battles with nature demons (i.e., dragons and the like) as a feature of classical matriarchal mythology.[18] This conclusion is certainly a questionable one for Mesopotamian myth, where the cosmic battle between the chaos-dragon Tiamat and the god-king Marduk represents not a development from goddess-centered mythology but a patriarchal rejection of the ancient goddess as the source of cosmic life. Others may be bothered not only by her historical reconstructions based on myth, but also by the political position which affirms mother-right and mother-rule without reflection on the possiblities of abuse inherent in any such system of gender dominance. However, Göttner-Abendroth does see matriarchal social organization as far more egalitarian and wholesome than any known to us under patriarchy, but once again, this is a very complex argument to sustain when based primarily on imaginative texts.[19]

The brief review of these models for evaluating the status of ancient women and the relationship of that status to the presence of goddesses and their worship leaves us with some directions for inquiry and cautions about how we proceed. As we turn to women's texts from the ancient world then, we must beware of the temptation of generalization. Status of elite, goddess-identified women (see Enheduanna and Puduhepa, below) may not extend to their lower-class sisters, nor should we assume that the presence of goddesses always implies a higher view of female authority and power. Questions of status should always be asked in conjunction with study of the economic power held by women. Future work should attempt to test Sanday's hypothesis about women's contribution to a culture's subsistence needs and the percentage of full-service goddesses in the society, although that is beyond the scope of the present essay. Further, in so far as possible given the texts with which we are working, we should attempt to press our questions about women's roles and status into the domestic sphere and not simply in the public domain where only a few exceptional women find a place. We should be alert to recurring patterns within the literature and cultures studied, while simultaneously resisting the easy assumption that a given motif or pattern will carry the same oncology and meaning in one culture as it does in another. Finally, we must be sensitive to the "literary" nature of the texts studied with respect to the proportion of cultural verisimilitude likely to be present, preferencing economic texts and correspondence, for example, more highly than tales and myths. With these injunctions in mind, let us now turn to the examination of texts by some ancient women of Mesopotamia and Anatolia.

"Be it known!": Ancient Women Speak

In the cuneiform sources reflecting the rise of the kingdom of Akkad in the last half of the third millennium we meet a truly remarkable woman: Enheduanna of Ur (ca. 2300-2230 BCE). Daughter of the great political leader Sargon of Akkad, Enheduanna combined the roles of princess, priestess, and poet to such an extent that centuries later her literary works were still being catalogued and held in great esteem by the cultures which had inherited them. One scholar has gone so far as to declare her the "first non-anonymous author in literature."[20]

The origins of her father Sargon, salient to our discussion here, have been mythologized: he claimed to be the son of the union between a high priestess and an unknown father. A water-drawer plucked him from the river where his mother had placed him after she secretly gave birth, and he later came into power when the goddess Ištar gave him her love as he worked as a gardener.[21] Some scholars take this to mean that he was aided by women, perhaps devotees of Ištar, in his rise to power. Subsequently, Sargon was able to unite the city-state kingdoms of Sumer (Ur and Uruk) with his own kingdom of Akkad. Several political and theological moves paved the way for and symbolized his consolidation of Sumerian and Akkadian culture. He appointed his daughter Enheduanna to a dual cultic role as high priestess-bride of the moongod Nanna in Ur and also installed her as a cultic functionary in Uruk, thus honoring the Sumerian traditions wherein a male deity was served by a female cult official or *en*, and vice versa. He synthesized Sumerian and Akkadian theologies by identifying his patron diety, the semitic Ištar, with the Sumerian Inanna.[22] In the masterful Sumerian poetic compositions of his daughter Enheduanna, this identification is carried through with style and fervor, and constitutes one of the world's first efforts at a "systematic theology." Enheduanna's life and work are known to us through her seals, inscriptions, and the cycle of hymns to Inanna and the temples of Sumer which comes from her hand or has been attributed to her. We have her portrait preserved on a badly damaged disc from Ur.[23]

In her composition *nin-me-šar-ra*, or "The Exaltation of Inanna" as it has come to be known, Enheduanna moves beyond a mere propagation of her father's political theology to a personal identification with the fortunes of her beloved goddess. The same terms used to depict Inanna's past flights from the cities of Sumer are employed to describe the usurper Lugalanna's expulsion of Enheduanna from her priestly offices in Ur and Uruk. When appeals to the moon god Nanna and the sky god An prove futile (since Lugalanna now controls their cults), she turns hopefully to Inanna. She says of her own composition that inspiration came to her at night and that she "gave birth" to this song, "that which I recited to you at (mid)night/May the singer repeat it to you at noon!" (lines 139–140).[24] By casting her predicament in terminology which has been applied to the goddess' own past trials, Enheduanna forges a bond of compassionate empathy by which she hopes to return to her former position of service to the goddess. Given the reconstructed political context which informs the composition, it is not surprising that it is the martial aspects of Inanna, rather than the fertility functions, which receive the most emphasis:

> That you are lofty as Heaven—be it known!
> That you are broad as the earth—be it known!
> That you devastate the rebellious land—be it known!
> That you roar at the land—be it known!
> That you smite the heads—be it known!
> That you devour cadavers like a dog—be it known!
> That your glance is terrible—be it known!
> That you lift your terrible glance—be it known!
> That your glance is flashing—be it known! . . .
> That you attain victory—it known! . . .
> Oh my lady beloved of An, I have verily recounted your fury!
>
> lines 123–130, 132, 135

Since the text considered here is a prayer text which contains clear liturgical elements ("be it known!"), it can be rated fairly high on our scale of verisimilitude. While Enheduanna certainly makes use of hymnic convention and hyperbole, both in the invocatory epithets and the "complaint" section which details her humiliation at the hands of the usurper, since she is seeking redress of tangible wrongs we must assume that her account and plea bear some clear relationship to the historic events that occasioned them. Like the individual complaint psalms of the Hebrew Bible, we may not know the precise details of what has afflicted the psalmist, but we are generally on safe ground in concluding that *something happened*. She who had "carried the ritual basket" and "intoned the acclaim" has been "placed in the lepers' ward" (lines 68–69).[26] Enheduanna had encountered the "catch-22" in the status of women "elites": where status derives from the politics and pleasures of one's male relatives, one can be easily "de-classed" when new elite males take charge. When the gods to whom she had been espoused turned a deaf ear to her lament, she turned to the goddess Inanna-Ištar with the cry "O my divine impetuous wild cow, drive out this man, capture this man!" (line 91).[27] If we are to believe the composition's concluding lines, the goddess did not desert her as had her gods. It may have been

Enheduanna's father who placed her in power, but it was her goddess who restored her and her own talents which insured her an enduring place in Sumerian literature.

"If truly you are my daughter . . ."

The opportunities and pitfalls associated with the role of princess in Mesopotamia are well attested in the literature from the city-state of Mari (Tell Hariri) in the Old Babylonian period.[28] During the reign of King Zimri-Lim (ca. 1780-1760 BCE, middle chronology) women in his court held a remarkable range of positions in both the public and private spheres. An able strategist, Zimri-Lim was often away from Mari while conducting his numerous campaigns to establish and maintain Mari's hegemony along the upper Euphrates. For this reason, he often had occasion to leave matters of state and religion in the capable hands of his head queen Šibtu, herself a princess from the court of Aleppo in Yamhad. It was there that she apparently met and married Zimri-Lim when he had fled Mari in exile at his father's death. Although he had many wives and a large harem, Šibtu clearly held a preeminent place in his affections and trust. Scholars speculate that since no such broad role for the queen or queen-mother was known in Mari either before or after Zimri-Lim's reign, that the extraordinary activity of the women in Zimri-Lim's family is an example of women claiming "unassigned power" when circumstances permit, rather than of any institutionalized "assigned power" in the city-state. Our main textual evidence for this period comes from correspondence from the royal archives.[29]

Šibtu's correspondence is quite varied, permitting some glimpses into personal life, even though most of it is economic and routine in nature, as she carries out tasks delegated to her by Zimri-Lim and updates him on the state of affairs in the palace and city. Much of the interchange between the pair which is private in nature consists of her inquiries about the king's health, reports of favorable omens which she had ordered taken for him, and his reassuring replies about his welfare and the fortunes of the army. In ARM X 26, she reports, "(To my lord) say: Thus Šibtu (your) maidservant: I have (just given) birth to twins—a son and a daughter. May my lord rejoice!"[30] Elsewhere (ARM X 17) she writes that she is sending Zimri-Lim a coat and other articles of clothing that she has made herself, requesting that he wear them. But apart from such typical domestic roles, Šibtu was involved in acting as an all-purpose factotum for her absent lord. She oversaw the direction of the palace, the harem, the temple, workshops, and the entire city, receiving and sending diplomatic correspondence to the outlying provinces, showing that her influence and authority extended well beyond the city of Mari itself. Aside from overseeing the city archives, she supervised the work of various officials, many of whom sought her influence in settling a variety of official and personal matters. She was also in contact with her father's court and acted to secure positive treatment for favorites. In the realm of cultic activity, she filled the role of king or governor as needed, escorting the cult statues, ordering sacrifices, and relaying divine oracles to the king.

That she was a concerned and thoughtful queen is evident from the number of appeals for help which she received and the letters from her which direct officials to give aid and comfort. In ARM X 153, one Kibri-Dagan was requested by her to discover what was causing a particular woman's "heartache"; in ARM X 160, she arranges for the release of women who had been given in pledge for a debt. In ARM X 114, Tarišhattu, a woman of higher rank (perhaps a widow of Zimri-Lim's father?), writes to Šibtu to settle a matter of slander, saying "If truly you are my daughter and you love my health, then you will convey (this matter) to the king. . . .[31]

Also evident from her letters is the fact that she had fully internalized the values of imperial patriarchy, among them the well-known "double-standard" that limits the sexual activity of women while allowing a full range of opportunities for men. So great is Zimri-Lim's trust in his queen's solidarity with his goals that he is able to direct her to select the most beautiful of the women taken in battle for his harem (ARM X 126), though he later decides to see to the matter himself. When an epidemic strikes the harem (X 129–130), it is Šibtu who carries out Zimri-Lim's instructions for limiting the spread of the disease.[32] From the correspondence available to us, we can conclude that Šibtu firmly understood that her welfare was tied to the fortunes of her lord; she does not grudge him a fine harem or lesser wives to oversee other palaces, for such arrangements were expected of a great king and testified to his prominence, hence augmenting her own. As is often seen in ethnographic data, a variety of factors determine whether or not the addition of another woman to the household is seen as threatening to personal status or as enhancing the available pool of workers.[33] The "other woman" only becomes a threat where the head wife's status or husband's affections are jeopardized by the addition of the new female—we may think here of the fates of Sarah and Leah in the biblical narratives. Unlike them, Šibtu, daughter of the powertul king of Yamḥad, was secure in her position and assured in her relationship with Zimri-Lim.

"Even if I am a woman . . ."

Not all of the princesses of Mari were so fortunate as Queen Šibtu and that we ought not to generalize from her position is brought home in letters concerning Zimri-Lim's daughters' struggles with their co-wives. Part of Zimri-Lim's plan for the maintenance of strong vassal alliances involved the giving of daughters in political marriages. Royal daughters in such positions also served their father by acting as trusted informants on political and socioeconomic conditions in their region, actions which predictably caused friction when vassal husbands were less than whole-hearted in their allegiance to Mari. One of Zimri-Lim's daughters, Inib-šarri, was given in marriage to Ibal-Addu of Ašlakka, only to discover, much to her dismay, that a previous wife still held the position of head-wife and queen (ARM X 74). After writing to Zimri-Lim concerning her husband's potentially traitorous activities, she flees to a neighboring city and writes her father entreating him to return her to Mari (ARM X 77, II 112, 113). While in "exile" in Naḥur, she corresponds with an official on various matters, at one point invoking the blessing of Belet-ekallim (=Ningal?), her goddess, to protect him (ARM X 78).[34] We do not know the outcome of her requests to return home.

Another daughter who was successful in achieving the dissolution of a noxious political marriage was Kiru, married to one Ḥaya-Sumu of Ilanṣura. Again, the father's political motives set the stage for the daughter's misery: Zimri-Lim had not only given Kiru in marriage but had also established her as mayor in her own right; at the same time, he gave Ḥaya-Sumu another (adoptive?) daughter, Šibatum, perhaps by a lesser ranking wife, and this is the queen favored by Ḥaya-Sumu. Domestic battles escalate among the trio, until Ḥaya-Sumu threatens Kiru's life (ARM X 32). Desperate, Kiru writes home to daddy: "If he (the king) does not bring me back, I shall die; I will not live," and again, "If my lord does not bring me back, I will head toward Mari (and there) jump (fall) from the roof" (ARM X 33). Humiliated before guests, deprived of her rightful servants and prerogatives, and finally threatened with death, Kiru's pleas were finally heard. In ARM X 135, Zimri-Lim instructs Šibtu to make arrangements to return Kiru to Mari.[35]

Other examples of unhappily married daughters of Zimri-Lim exist, but not all marriages ended so unfortunately as Kiru's and Inib-šarri's. Other daughters found sufficient happiness in their politically motivated marriages to write to Zimri-Lim on their husbands' behalf (ARM X 98). At least one daughter was sent into the cloister as a *nadītu*-woman (ARM X 38), and we also hear the daughters of other kings mentioned in the Mari correspondence. While Zimri-Lim did not hesitate to make use of his daughters as instruments of foreign policy, he maintained contact with them although we may wonder how much of his correspondence was due to fatherly affection since the information obtained by his daughters was of great benefit to his own political maneuvering. Indeed, Kiru even writes Zimri-Lim reminding him of previous problems caused when he disregarded her reports (ARM X 31), concluding "And now, even if I am a woman, may my father and lord listen to my message."[36] Still, Zimri-Lim sought to influence the fate of his daughters for the good, occasionally even giving them assigned powers within the political structure. But if the rank of princess could bequeath special status and opportunities to a woman like Šibtu, it is clear it could also bring considerable hazards as in the cases of Kiru and Inib-šarri. Once again, the fate of royal women, like that of their lower-class sisters, was almost entirely dependent on the wishes and whims of the men who controlled their lives.

In the realm of religion, we are given intriguing hints from the Mari letters about how women related to the gods and goddesses of their regions. Women are often found offering prayers before the gods Šamas, Adad, and Dagan for the safety of the king and his armies. Women also offer sacrifices, commission oracles and are found worshiping both the main gods of Mari, Dagan and Adad, as well as other gods (Šamas, Itur-Mer, Nanna, Tešub, etc.) and the goddesses of their own and surrounding areas (Ištar, Ištar.RA.DA.NA, Annunitum, Ḫebat, Belet-ekallim). Women served as lay and professional prophetesses for both gods and goddesses, and could be attached to specific cult centers (including cloisters) in a variety of capacities. While such a dedication provided status and authority to the women involved, it offered only moderate protection in time of war: in ARM X 126, we learn that some *ugbabātum*-priestesses were taken as war captives, but were not forced into the textile factories as slave labor as the other female captives were.[37]

Two tantalizingly brief events relating women to their goddesses might be mentioned. In ARM X 87, one Šattamkiyazi has left her own city to serve the king in another, apparently against the wish of her goddess, Ištar.RA.DA.NA, as expressed in a liver omen. As a consequence, she has become quite ill ("the hand of Ištar.RA.DA.NA presses heavily against me"), and requests leave of the king to offer another sacrifice to her goddess in hope of restoring her health.[38] In ARM X 112, women servants of the palace tell the male palace servants that "we are constantly praying for you to Belet-ekallim."[39] While the evidence from Mari does not permit us to conclude that it was the presence of goddesses there that accounted for the relatively high status of elite women and widespread activities of women in the cult, it is clear that women had deeply-felt "personal" relationships with their deities, goddesses as well as gods, and in official capacities could be regarded as legitimate representatives of the divine before the king, and vice versa.

"A Heifer from Thy Stable": Women of Anatolia

From the royal archives at Ḫattuša, capital of the Hittite empire which flourished in central Anatolia during the Late Bronze Age (ca. 1450-1200 BCE), comes a wealth of materials which shed light on the position of women in this most sophisticated of conqueror-kingdoms. Since space does not permit a thorough review of all the materials found at Ḫattuša, we will concentrate on two figures which represent the far ends of the social scale: Queen Puduḫepa and the MI.ŠU.GI of Hittite ritual texts.

Queen Puduḫepa was the wife and consort of Ḫattušili III, an able military and political leader who came to the throne through the irregular process of deposing his nephew. Ḫattušili later explains with some piety that this was all the idea of his personal goddess, Ištar of Šamuḫa, whom he was bound to obey since she had saved his life when he was only a sickly child. When the same Ištar told him to take Puduḫepa, a girl half his age, as wife, he naturally obeyed. That Puduḫepa was the daughter of a priest of Ištar in the southern province of Kizzuwatna, possibly of royal extraction, but certainly in a position to consolidate allegiances to the Hittites in a territory notable for its Hurrian and Mitannian ties only made obedience to the goddess that much more satisfying. The marriage was apparently a happy and fruitful one: Puduḫepa bore four children that are known, and her prayers and intercessions for Ḫattušili's health in his old age suggest that her relationship to her husband was a positive and fulfilling one. Due to the peculiarities of Hittite succession in the Old Kingdom, the Queen (-Mother) retained a powerful position even after the death of her husband, and Puduhepa continues to be mentioned during the reign of her son, Tudhaliya IV.[40]

Because of her mention in her husband's "Apology" and the many vows, prayer-texts and items of personal correspondence to and from the Hittite court, we know more about Puduhepa than any other woman of the Late Bronze Age. Although Hittite queens were always active in the religious sphere through their position as high priestess of the cult of the Sun-goddess of Arinna, the head of the Hittite pantheon, Puduhepa expanded her activities into the political and social realms. She had her own seal, carried on her own diplomatic correspondence, took a hand in arranging the settlements for her daughters in their political marriages (one married to Ramesses II, the other to the prince of Amurru), and is the only woman of the ancient world known to have received a divine "message" dream (as opposed to the "symbolic" dreams usually recorded for women).[41] She had her own chariot, probably to rush her to her cultic duties throughout the kingdom, and had access to temple treasuries, though she could not collect taxes. She carried out normal cultic and administrative duties associated with her rank, even took part in a court case (which was highly unusual in Hittite legal proceedings), and ordered materials from her home province of Kizzuwatna copied and archived in Ḫattuša.[42]

In the realm of personal theology, this queen left us materials which allow a glimpse into the religious sensibilities of a Bronze Age woman. Puduhepa's seal, like those of the Hittite kings and queens before her, shows her clasped in the embrace of the Sun-goddess of Arinna whose high-priestess she was. Both females wear strikingly similar costumes, and the seal reads GEME.DINGIR.LIM, "the servant of the goddess."[43] In KUB XXI, 27 Puduhepa addresses this goddess to plead for the restoration of her husband's health. The tone of her prayer is intimate, persuasive, and trusting. She tells the goddess

To the Sun-goddess of Arinna, my lady, the mistress of the Hatti lands, the queen of heaven and earth. Sun-goddess of Arinna, thou art queen of all countries! In the Hatti country thou bearest the name of the Sun-goddess of Arinna; but in the land which thou madest the cedar land thou bearest the name Hebat. I, Pudu-hepas, am a servant of thine from of old, a heifer from thy stable, a foundation stone (upon which) thou (canst rest). Thou, my lady, rearedst me and Hattušilis, thy servant to whom thou espousedst me, was closely associated with the Storm-god of Nerik, thy beloved son. . . .[44]

A number of features are of interest here. Puduḥepa, whose name means "Servant of Ḥebat," has made a clear connection between her patron goddess Ḥebat, a Hurrian mother goddess worshiped in her native "cedar" land,[45] and the Hattic mother-goddess (probably to be identified as Wuru(n)šemu) who heads the official Hittite pantheon. She further goes on to identify this Ḥebat/Wuru(n)šemu as the goddess who gave her in marriage to Ḥattušili, even though his "Apology" clearly states that it was Ištar of Šamuḫa who did so. In another portion of the "Apology" (12, ll. 7–15), we learn of one of Puduḥepa's dreams:

> Now, while My Lady Ishtar had even before this been promising me the kingship, at that time My Lady Ishtar appeared to my wife in a dream: "I shall march before your husband. And all Hattušas shall be led with your husband. Since I thought highly of him, I did not—no, not ever—abandon him to the hostile trial, the hostile deity." Now also I will exalt him, and make him priest of the sun goddess of Arinnas. Do you also make me, Ishtar, (your) patron deity."[46]

Since the prayer of Puduḥepa cited above (KUB XXI, 27) is usually dated toward the end of Ḥattušili's reign, we presume here that the dream appearance of Ištar occurred earlier since it is clearly narrated as taking place before Ḥattušili's seizure of the throne. Has Puduḥepa taken her husband's Ištar as her patron deity, thus fusing this militant goddess with the mother-goddesses of her youth and her official cultic roles? Though modern scholars are often apt to separate the military roles of the nubile "maiden" goddess from the nurturing roles of the "mother" goddess, it is clear that such distinctions did not hold for at least one ancient devotee.

Like Enheduanna's fusion of the Sumerian Inanna and the Semitic Ištar, Puduḥepa's thealogical move here can be understood as growing out of her experience of her goddesses. Both thealogical and political motivations are at work. The Hittites of the New Kingdom were known for their syncretistic policies which incorporated the deities of conquered territories into the official pantheon rather than repressing indigenous worship. They were self-styled as "people of the thousand gods," and indeed, it seems they never met a diety they didn't like, which resulted in a cultic calendar so ridiculously full that wars had to be interrupted so that the king could perform his assorted ritual duties. Hence, Puduḥepa's syncretism takes place against a background of easy tolerance and official approval. While it is not too far a "stretch" to identify Ḥebat with the Sun-goddess of Arinna since they are both understood as consorts of the Weather-god of Ḫatti and mothers of the divine son, the Weather-god of Nerik (the Hurrian Šarruma), the immediate coherence between these mother figures and the battle-ready Ištar, the Weather-god's sister, is not so readily apparent. Politically, it was important that the official head of the Hittite pantheon, the Sun-goddess of Arinna, accept Ḫattušili, the favorite of Ištar, as an acceptable if irregular king. Puduḫepa's syncretism allows this by identifying the goddess who brought her husband to power with the goddess who sustains and authorizes Hittite kingship.[47] But the Queen's consolidation of these divine females moves beyond simple pragmatic politics into the realm of faith—could the power that moved her from her home into an unknown land actually be any different from the loving power she knew as a child and continued to experience as queen? Puduḫepa's Hurrian roots have been posited as an explanation of the marked Hurrian-Hittite theological syncretism during Ḫattušili's reign, though the beginning of this trend can be traced back further. However, it is to the common condition of women that we must turn for the deeper psychological motivation behind the politics. Like the royal daughters of Sumer and Mari, Puduḫepa probably had very little choice in her marriage partner or place of residence. Dedicated to Ḫebat by her very name, it is scarcely possible that a woman of faith would leave her native deities behind, and highly probable that she would identify the divine figures with whom she was familiar with those who populated her new world. Where women are moved and traded like game-pieces on the board of political hegemony, they cannot afford inflexible deities bound to a given location. The goddesses a woman worshiped had to be thealogically "portable" if they were to be of any use to the devotee—a goddess only effective in the "Cedar Land" was of limited value to the Queen in Ḫattuša. As Puduḫepa grew, changed residence and social rank, her understanding of her goddess grew and traveled along with her. She can speak of herself as "a heifer from thy stable," a "foundation stone (upon which) thou (canst rest)," both metaphors which conjure up images of service, dedication, and long-term intimacy. Later in her prayer Puduḫepa goes on to draw parallels between the motherhood of the Sun-goddess and her own travail over Ḫattušili's illness. In a culture obsessed by ritual purity, Puduḫepa can speak to her divine helper using images drawn from the world of women, from the time when a woman's body is presented in all its primal "otherliness" and potential impurity, and be guaranteed a positive hearing not in spite of her sex *but because of it*, since this gender marking is shared with the goddess. A reader of the biblical book of Leviticus can conceive of such a relationship between women and the exclusive male god of ancient Israel only with the greatest of difficulty, though to be sure, the female characters of the Bible are often presented as relating their birth-giving activities in some way to that same god they are not allowed to approach.[48]

"I am speaking the gods' words . . ."

A fascinating look at the role certain females might play that crosses the boundaries between the public and private domains can be found in the recorded rituals of the MI.ŠU.GI (Hittite: MI.ḫašauwaš), or "old women."[49] These women constitute the class of practitioners most often mentioned in Hittite ritual texts, and were truly indispensable to the functioning of that society. Many of the rituals by them are recorded in the first person, so we have a sense of a qualified informant bequeathing her "recipe" for the restoration of health, purity and peace to the tradition for use in similar circumstance. Many of these women appear to be from the provinces of Kizzuwatna and Arzawa, and the Hurrian element in these rituals is especially pronounced.[50] An Old Kingdom edict of Ḫattušili I aims at curtailing the influence of the MI.ŠU.GI on the women of the palace, and it has been suggested that they, along with the Hattic city elders and the Tawananna (the king's wife in Hittite times, but originally the king's *sister* and mother of the heir-presumptive in the Hattic period), represented one of the indigenous groups attempting to resist the imposition of cultural changes brought by the Indo-European Hittite conquerors.[51] We know the names of thirteen women designated as MI.ŠU.GI, with many other women appearing as "authors" of magical rituals whom scholars also consider to be recognized practitioners.[52] Among these, the proposed MI.ŠU.GI Ayatarša is said to be the female slave of one Nawila; one Anniwiyani is called "mother of Armatis, the bird-maker, slave of Hurlus," so that we know that MI.ŠU.GI were not cloistered as the *nadītu* were.[53] Here, then, we have an exception which tests the rule by which modern scholars usually assume that slave-women are necessarily women of low status. The Hittite MI.ŠU.GI was endowed with powers so formidable that kings must legislate against them and tradition must encode her words, and yet she could be owned by another.

The MI.ŠU.GI performed her services in a number of areas. The rituals with whose authorship she is credited or those which may reasonably be attributed to her include evocation magic (calling enemy gods away from their towns and calling native gods back to their own place), countermagic against sorcery, removal of ritual impurity and quarrels, restoration of sexual functions, the healing of children, the interpretation of omens, and royal funerary rites.[54] An example of how authoritative were her words and actions comes from the preamble of Annanna's *mugawar* ritual designed to entice the Sungod's return to his own land: "I am speaking the gods' words and am evoking him" (VBoT 58 iv 9-10).[55] A full picture of the sphere of her activities emerges from a reading of the variety of rituals recorded. She selected rituals appropriate for a given situation, assembled or created necessary equipment (wax and clay figures, woolen thread, household items, food and drink, wooden pegs, stones, mud, herbs, dung), gave orders, made sacrifices, interpreted omens, and pronounced words of blessing and curse. She most frequently called upon the Sungod in her rituals, but invoked other deities as necessary for the given situation. She speaks decisively when her rituals are recorded, and her words and deeds were obviously considered efficacious enough to be recorded for posterity. An excerpt from the Ritual of Tunnawi gives some of the flavor of her words and deeds:

> If a person, either a man or a woman, has been placed in any impurity, or someone else has named him/her for impurity, or (if) her children repeatedly die within the woman, or (if) her children are born prematurely, or (if) in a man or woman the sexual organs are disabled as a result of a formula of impurity, and that person is experiencing impurity, then that person, whether a man or woman, performs the ritual of impurity. . . .[56]

After various hex-breaking activities, she recites the incantation "Evil impurity, witchcraft, sin, anger of the god, terror of the dead, the wickedness of mankind, remove (all) that!"[57] Although the Hittite's possessed other male and female ritual practitioners and physician-priests, it was the work of the MI.ŠU.GI which was most frequently called upon by society.[58]

"I am at peace and sisterly": Letters from Egypt

From the Hittite royal archives found at Boghazkoy also comes evidence of the correspondence carried on between "Naptera" (=Nefertari), the Great Royal Wife of Ramesses II, and "Petkhep" (=Puduhepa) of Hattiland. After Ramesses and Ḥattušili (then

serving his brother, the king Muwatalli) fought one another over
Syrian hegemony at the battle of Kadesh (ca. 1286/85) with the Egyptian army only narrowly escaping an ignominious defeat at the hands
of the Hittites, the two nations sought to come to agreement by treaty
(ca. 1271) rather than through clash of arms. As usual, the agree-
ments of nations were sealed "with a kiss"—by the exchange of
appropriate females. In this case, M3'T-HR-NFRW-R' ("Justice is the
beautiful face of God (Re)"), the daughter of Puduhepa and Hattušili
was given to Ramesses as a wife, and the letters (KBo I 29; KBo I 21?)
passing between to the two queens seem related to this occasion.[59]
As was noted in the correspondence between Šibtu and Zimri-Lim,
the head wife has little concern over the double standard which provides her husband with many wives as a political matter of course.
Nefertari writes in response to Puduhepa's routine inquiry over her
health, and speaks of the "good brotherhood" which Re, the Sungod,
will give to Hattušili and Ramesses. For her own part, she says "And
I am at peace and sisterly with the great queen, my sister; I, now (and
forever)."[60]

Along with these treaty texts comes an interesting reflection of the
"gender" question regarding deities. The Egyptian copy of "Hittite
treaty" contains a notice describing the seal of Puduhepa which the
treaty bears. The Egyptian scribe wrote

> Female figure in the likeness of (the great goddess) of the Khatti,
> clasping in her arms the figure of the Great Queen of Khatti. Circum-
> scription: Seal of the Sun-god of the city of Arenna, (A-r-n-na) lord of
> the land; seal of Putu-khipa, Great Queen of Khatti, daughter of the
> land of Kizawaden, mistress (?) of the city of Arenna, mistress of the
> land, the ministress of the goddess. In the border: the seal of the Sun-
> god of Arenna, the lord of all the land.[61]

This is actually an excellent description of Puduhepa's seal, known
to us from other archaeological finds, but it seems clear that the Egyptian scribe, undoubtedly male, felt some confusion. In Egypt, the
solar deity was clearly male, yet in Hatti, a different gender tradition
about this deity obtains. While the scribe has dutifully described the
goddess who clasps Puduhepa, he has had trouble incorporating this
female deity into his traditional theological language, choosing
instead to translate by using the typical solar disc hieroglyph which
stands for Re. While some scholars argue that this means that the
hieroglyph must therefore carry an androgynous meaning, it also
seems likely that the scribe, even while recording the outlandish
Hittite view, reinforced his notion that the solar deity was male. That

the disputes over appropriate gender designations for deity began at least as early as the Late Bronze Age should afford modern persons engaged in that struggle some comfort: obviously, these are not easy questions to decide.

Conclusion: Syncretistic Thealogy

In closing, this brief glimpse into the words and lives of ancient women has brought us closer to an understanding of the conditions that bounded their lives, and shown us the strength and wit with which they addressed and expanded the roles decreed for them by society. It was impossible to speak of the lives of these women, mostly elites, without also speaking of the menfolk to whom they were attached. Where we had access to the personal feelings of these women, we saw head wives generally content with their lot, and more attached to their men than to the less fortunate women, occasionally even their daughters, who surrounded them. Slavery was accepted as a matter of course; sexual exploitation of captives was regarded as routine. Women caught up in struggles with their co-wives or in conflict with elite males outside their kinship group seemed more conscious of their lower status as female, but even so, this concern did not extend to women of lower classes who frequently appear as pawns traded in the battle for prestige. Few women of other-than-elite status were available for study, due to the nature of the materials available.[62]

At least some of the women considered here could be designated as "goddess-identified," particularly Enheduanna, Šattamkiyazi, and Puduhepa. In each case, the affiliation served as a basis for at least some of the high status each was accorded, and this, in turn, was tied into the political fortunes reflected in worship of that goddess. In the contexts where a relationship between women and the status-authorizing goddess could be discerned, the women in question also seemed fully engaged, at least in an administrative way, in the economic life of the temple, city-state or kingdom in question, providing tentative support for Sanday's hypothesis.

A particular trend toward syncretism was recognized, in service of both politics and female religious sensibilities. Enheduanna could fuse the Sumerian Inanna to the Semitic Ištar; Puduhepa found the goddess of her "Cedar Land" alive and well in the cult center of Arinna, and identified both with her husband's patron goddess.

Egyptian women's names also reflect a similar syncretizing perspective: the Egyptian name of Puduḥepa's daughter identified the goddess "Ma'at," or "Justice" as the beautiful face of the sungod Re; the throne name of Hatshepsut, M3'T-K3-R', makes a similar move, proclaiming "Justice (Ma'at) is the likeness of God (Re)." We might also think here of the Egyptian maidservant Hagar, who is narratively the first to identify the Hebrew patriarchal God-of-the-fathers with one of the indigenous gods of Canaan (Gen 16:13-14). As the women were moved from place to place, they found that their deities moved with them, and though both might acquire new names, the relationship of mutuality remained undisturbed.[63]

NOTES

1. J. Mellaart, *Čatal Hüyük* (London: Thames & Hudson, 1967) 101; "Excavations at Catal Hüyük, 1963: Third Preliminary Report," *Anatolian Studies* XIV (1964) 93.

2. The latest entry in the popular literature about Crete may be found in R. Eisler, *The Chalice and the Blade: Our History, Our Future* (San Francisco: Harper & Row, 1987) 29–41. For a critique of this popular view of the Minoans, see C. G. Starr, "Minoan Flower Lovers," *The Minoan Thalassocracy: Myth and Reality*, ed. R. Hagg and N. Marinator (Stockholm: Proc. Third International Symposium at the Swedish Institute in Athens, 31 May-5 June, 1982) 9-12.

3. C. J. Bleeker, "Isis and Hathor: Two Ancient Egyptian Goddesses," *The Book of the Goddess: Past and Present*, ed. C. Olson (New York: Crossroad, 1985) 29–48; J. Ochshorn, "Ishtar and Her Cult," Olson, *Goddess* 16–28. Obviously, phrasing comments on historical goddess cults in this way has already injected a modern perspective into our interpretation.

4. G. Greene and C. Kahn, "Feminist Scholarship and the Social Construction of Woman," *Making a Difference: Feminist Literary Criticism*, ed. G. Greene and C. Kahn (New York: Methuen, 1985) 18.

5. Jonathan Culler, *The Pursuit of Signs: Semiotics, Literature, Deconstruction* (Ithaca: Cornell Univ., 1981) 3-17.

6. M. Bal, *Lethal Love: Feminist Literary Readings of Biblical Love Stories* (Bloomington: Indiana Univ., 1987) 132.

7. R. Jacobsen, "Closing Statement: Linguistics and Poetics," *Style in Language*, ed. T. A. Sebeok (Cambridge, MA: M.I.T., 1960) 350-77; T. Hawkes, *Structuralism and Semiotics* (Berkeley: Univ. of California, 1977) 76-87.

8. Inscriptions from Ramesses II claimed that he won the battle of Kadesh against the Hittites. He lied: at the very least, it must be considered a draw, if not an actual Hittite victory. See below.

9. For a discussion of the use of comparative ethnographic data, see R. R. Wilson, *Genealogy and History in the Biblical World* (New Haven: Yale Univ. Press, 1977).

10. T. F. Carney, *The Shape of the Past: Models and Antiquity* (Lawrence, KS: Corondao, 1975) 149; C. Meyers, *Discovering Eve: Ancient Israelite Women in Context* (New York: Oxford Univ. Press, 1988) 139-57.

11. M. T. Whyte, *The Status of Women in Preindustrial Societies* (Princeton: Princeton Univ., 1978) 170; for an assessment of how women's class affiliation is derived from the men to whom they are attached, see G. Lerner, *The Creation of Patriarchy* (New York: Oxford Univ. Press, 1986) 9.

12. Whyte, *Status* 13-26.

13. Whyte, *Status* 167-84.

14. *Woman, Culture & Society*, ed. M. Z. Rosaldo and L. Lamphere (Stanford, CA: Stanford Univ., 1974) 189-206.

15. Sanday, "Female Status" 198-200.

16. Sanday, "Female Status" 203-206.

17. J. Hackett, "Can a Sexist Model Liberate Us? Ancient Near Eastern "Fertility" Goddesses," *JFSR* forthcoming. For an analysis of the different roles filled by "fertility" deities, see J. Ochshorn, *The Female Experience and the Nature of the Divine* (Bloomington: Indiana Univ. Press, 1981).

18. Göttner-Abendroth, *Göttin* 118.

19. Göttner-Abendroth, *Göttin* 12-16.

20. W. W. Hallo, "Women of Sumer," *The Legacy of Sumer, BibMesop* 4, ed. D. Schmandt-Besserat (Malibu, CA: Undena, 1976) 29.

21. E. A. Speiser, tr., "The Legend of Sargon," *Ancient Near Eastern Texts Relating to the Old Testament*, 3rd. ed. with Supplement, ed. J. B. Pritchard (Princeton: Princeton Univ. Press, 1969 = ANET) 119.

22. For a fuller portrait of the character of Inanna, see my study, "The Deceptive Goddess in Ancient Near Eastern Myth: Inanna and Inaraš," *Semeia* 42 (1988) 87-93.

23. W. W. Hallo and J. J. A. Van Dijk, *The Exaltation of Inanna, YNER* 3 (New Haven: Yale Univ. Press, 1968) 1-11. *contra* J. Ochshorn, "Mothers and Daughters in Ancient Near Eastern Literature," *The Lost Tradition: Mothers and Daughters in Literature* (ed. C. N. Davidson and E. M. Broner; New York: Frederick Ungar, 1980) 7; Enheduanna writes in Sumerian, not Akkadian.

24. Hallo and Van Dijk, *Exaltation* 33.

25. Hallo and Van Dijk, *Exaltation* 31-32.

26. Hallo and Van Dijk, *Exaltation* 23.

27. Hallo and Van Dijk, *Exaltation* 27.

28. For an English introduction to the materials from Mari, see *BA* 47 (1984) which is devoted to this topic.

29. G. Dossin, *Archives royales de Mari, X: La correspondence féminine* (Paris: Département des Antiquités Orientales, Textes cunéiformes, XXXI, Musée du Louvre, 1967) = ARM X; W. H. Ph. Römer, *Frauenbriefe über Religion, Politik und Privatleben in Mari: Untersuchungen zu. G. Dossin, Archives Royales de Mari*

X (Paris 1967), *AOAT* 12 (Neukirchen-Vluyn, 1971); B. F. Batto, *Studies on Women at Mari* (Baltimore: Johns Hopkins Univ., 1974); P. Artzi and A. Malamat, "The Correspondence of Šibtu, Queen of Mari in ARM X," *Or*, n.s., 40 (1971) 75–89; J. M. Sasson, "Biographical Notices on Some Royal Ladies from Mari," *JCS* 25 (1973) 59–78.

30. Artzi and Malamat, "Correspondence" 81.

31. Artzi and Malamat, "Correspondence" 78–79.

32. Batto, *Studies* 27–28.

33. L. Lamphere, "Strategies, Cooperation, and Conflict Among Women in Domestic Groups," *Women, Culture, Society* 97–112.

34. Batto, *Studies* 37–42, 131; Sasson, "Notices" 63–67.

35. Batto, *Studies* 42–48; Sasson, "Notices" 68–72.

36. Sasson, "Notices" 68.

37. Batto, *Studies* 79–139. Many of the women found in the service of the deities were elites, judging by their genealogical ties; where relationships to males are not mentioned it is difficult to decide whether or not lower-class women were involved in cult and religion in anything other than menial capacities.

38. Batto, *Studies* 128–29; Römer, *Frauenbriefe* 31.

39. Batto, *Studies* 131.

40. For Ḫattušili's version of the truth, see "The Apology of Hattusili III" in E. H. Sturtevant and G. Bechtel, *A Hittite Chrestomathy* (Philadelphia: Univ. of Penn. Press, 1935) 65–83. For a fuller discussion of Puduḫepa's career, see the present writer's "Queenly Proverb Performance: The Prayer of Puduḫepa (KUB XXI, 27)," *The Listening Heart: Essays in Wisdom and the Psalms in honor of Roland E. Murphy, O.Carm.*, ed. K. G. Hoglund, E. F. Huwiler, J. T. Glass and R. W. Lee (Sheffield, U.K.: JSOT Press, 1987; JSOT Supp 58) 95–126, and H. Otten, *Puduhepa: Eine hethitische Königin in ihren Textzeugnissen* (Mainz: Franz Steiner, 1975).

41. A. L. Oppenheim, *The Interpretations of Dreams in the Ancient Near East: With a Translation of an Assyrian Dream-Book* (Philadelphia: American Philosophical Society, 1956 = *Trans. Amer. Philosophical Soc.* 46/3) 254–55.

42. M. Darga, "Puduhepa: An Anatolian Queen of the Thirteenth Century B.C.," *Mansel'e Armagan: Mélanges Mansel = Festschrift Arif Müfid Mansel* (Ankara: Turk Tarih Kurumu Basimevi, 1974) 2:944–45; I. Seibert, *Woman in Ancient Near East*, rev. G. Shepperson (Leipzig: Edition Leipzig, 1974) 47–49.

43. S. R. Bin-Nun, *The Tawananna in the Hittite Kingdom* (Texte der Hethiter 5; Heidelberg: Carl Winter, 1975) 193. For a picture of Puduḫepa's seal, see E. Akurgal, *The Art of the Hittites* (New York: Harry Abrams, 1962).

44. A. Goetze, "Prayer of Pudu-hepas to the Sun-goddess of Arinna and her Circle," *ANET* 393. KUB = *Keilschriften aus Boghazöi*, I–XX V (Berlin, 1921–24).

45. For Hebat's association with the biblical "Eve" (Ḫawwat), see V. Haas, *Hethitische Berggötter und Hurritische Steindämonen: Riten, Kulte und Mythen* (Kulturgeschichte der antiken Welt 10; Mainz: Philipp von Zabern, 1982) 30.

46. Sturtevant and Bechtel, *Chrestomathy* 79.

47. It should be noted, however, that elsewhere it is the Weather-god who commissions the king, and that the Sun-goddess of Arinna is absent from foreign treaties, but see discussion of Puduḫepa's seal by Egyptian scribes, below. Bin-Nun, *Tawananna* 203–204.

48. Gen 4:1; 21:1; 25:21; 29:31; Ruth 4:13; 1 Sam 1:19–20, 27; 1 Sam 2:1–10; Luke 1.

49. O. R. Gurney, *Some Aspects of Hittite Religion* (Oxford: Oxford Univ. Press, 1976) 44–45.

50. Gurney, *Aspects*, 44; D. H. Englehard, "Hittite Magical Practices: An Analysis," (Ph.D. dissertation, Brandeis Univ., 1970) 13.

51. Bin-Nun, *Tawananna* 120–40.

52. Gurney, *Aspects*, 45, n. 2. Designated as MI.ŠU.GI are Annanna, Ḫebattarakki, Kueša, Malli, Mallidunna, Šilalluhi, Šušumanniga and Tunnawiya; Allaiduraḫi, Alli, Anniwiyani, Maštikka, and Paškuwatti are referred to by the variant SAL.ŠU.GI.

53. Englehard, "Practices" 23; Sturtevant and Bechtel, *Chrestomathy* 107.

54. Englehard, "Practices" 6–24.

55. Cited in Englehard, "Practices" 11; VBoT = *Verstreute Boghazköi-Texte* (Marburg, 1930).

56. Englehard, "Practices" 72.

57. Englehard, "Practices" 74.

58. Englehard, "Practices" 7.

59. D. D. Luckenbill, "Hittite Treaties and Letters," *AJSL* 37 (1921) 194. KBo = *Keilschrifttexte aus Boghazköi*, Hefte 1–6 (Leipzig, 1916–23), Hefte 7–17 (Berlin, 1954-).

60. Luckenbill, "Treaties" 194.

61. J. Garstang, "The Sun-Goddess of Arinna," *Annals of Archaeology and Anthropology* 6 (1914) 109.

62. Slave-women do appear as literary "types" in various biblical and extrabiblical narratives and instructions. A further analysis of the literary use to which they are put will appear in *Holy Torch of Heaven: Goddesses, Queens and Ordinary Women in the Ancient Near East*, in progress.

63. The research presented here is an excerpt from my forthcoming book, *Holy Torch of Heaven: Goddesses, Queens and Ordinary Women in the Ancient Near East*. The study was made possible by a sabbatical grant from Andover Newton Theological School spent as a Visiting Research Scholar in the Near Eastern and Jewish Studies Department of Brandeis University. I wish to thank Dorothy Moore, Deborah Vickers, Gerry Brague, Cara Davis, and Connie Schütz for their technical assistance in the preparation of this manuscript.

Human Persons as Images of the Divine:[1] A Reconsideration

ELLEN M. ROSS
Boston College

> Then God said, "Let us make the human person ['*adam*]
> in our image, after our likeness" (Genesis 1:26).

Introduction

WHAT USE HAVE feminist theologians for a concept that characterizes human persons as imitators of a God who is often
portrayed as a male deity?[2] What use have we for a description of the
human person which has been at times applied in a primary way to
males and only derivatively or secondarily to females?[3] Some may
say that we would do well to abandon the scriptural theme of
"human persons' creation in God's image" because the history of its
use has been resistant to the affirmation of women's full humanity.
I want to suggest something quite different here. By engaging in
dialogue with the writings of two medieval theologians of the Augustinian tradition, Richard of St. Victor (12th cent.) and Walter Hilton
(14th cent.), and the contemporary theologies of Rosemary Radford
Ruether and Dorothee Soelle, I will argue for the wisdom of recon-
sidering this central concept of the Christian tradition, suggesting
that the heritage of what this symbol has meant to Christian believers
may yet proffer theological guidance to communities of renewal and
hope in the late twentieth-century.

Both Richard of St. Victor, a theologian and mystic at the Abbey of
St. Victor in Paris, and Walter Hilton, an English spiritual guide,
were members of the Augustinians, a religious order of the high

Middle Ages that sought a middle way between the monastic life of cloistered nuns and monks, and the individualistic parish life of priests. For these two spiritual theologians, representative of one major type of medieval formulation of the *imago Dei* concept, the implications of the image theme are largely practical, operational, and moral: our identification as image-bearers applies not only to a past, creative association with God, nor only forward to a future, eschatological situation, but provides orienting and directive guidance in our day-to-day living with other bearers of the divine image.[4]

In conversation with Richard of St. Victor and Walter Hilton, I will argue for the centrality of the image of God theme in a contemporary feminist theology, suggesting that it is precisely the practical or moral implications of image-bearing that can be most helpful to theology today. In this vein I will consider the work of Rosemary Radford Ruether and of Dorothee Soelle who, for differing but complementary reasons, provide excellent resources for articulating a systematic and inclusive understanding of our identities as image-bearers. Ruether, who gives explicit attention to the *imago Dei* theme, is a feminist theologian committed to retrieving the scriptural message and affirming its transmission in the Christian tradition. Although critical of the Christian tradition's distortions of the message, Ruether is unwilling to dismiss Christianity's theological heritage completely, but prefers to draw selectively and constructively from it and from other disciplines and thought traditions in order to enrich contemporary theological reflection. The German theologian Dorothee Soelle, who speaks eloquently to the need for development of the interior life as the only possible cure to the social ills afflicting the contemporary world, makes little direct use of the image of God theme. But her lengthy discussions of the motifs related to it, and in particular, her analysis of the "sins" or "vices" of our time, makes her a valuable resource. Soelle provides a contemporary analysis of what Hilton would call "the image of sin," our dissimilarity to God, and a vision of solidarity, an affirmation of the unalterable connection between love of God and love of neighbor.

In considering Ruether and Soelle as representatives of prevalent tendencies within feminist theology, I will indicate how the image of God theme as described by the two medieval Augustinian canons might complement and enrich feminist theologians' affirmations of our full humanity and call for a holistic, developmental way of being which invites the use of all our human faculties in a socially responsible context. The image of God theme as set forth by Richard of St. Victor and Walter Hilton provides a rich symbol of the "thinking-relational"[5] self both Ruether and Soelle help us to recover. In particular, I will suggest that the contribution of medieval reflection on the image to contemporary theology arises from (1) its depiction of the human person as constituted in a fundamental way by its relationship to the Divine; (2) its analysis of the importance of personal and social transformation in our lives; and (3) its offering of language and imagery to express our intimacy with God and the world.

In the dialectic between medieval and contemporary feminist theology, feminist thought, for its part, introduces themes that highlight dimensions of the image concept which were unexplored during the Middle Ages; specifically, I will point to feminist theology's major role in recognizing the implications of the image of God theme for shaping our political experience. Despite significant differences in style and method—Ruether more concerned with reclaiming the systematic structure of the Christian tradition, and Soelle with rejuvenating the spiritual life of her audiences—Ruether and Soelle are united in their concern to celebrate the dignity of the human person in relationship to God and the world and to celebrate the possibilities of the Christian tradition. And like much of contemporary theology which focusses on the political ramifications of theological expression,[6] the theologies of both Soelle and Ruether are explicitly political and economic insofar as theological claims have praxis implications that call for concrete responses. While precedents for these concerns are not readily apparent in the political claims of medieval thinkers like Richard and Hilton, we can find a compatible sensibility in the significant social dimensions of theology evident, for example, in Richard and Hilton's identification of love with mutual interaction of love of God and neighbor, and not exclusively— with either love of self or love of God. As Richard puts it, for us to attain love in its highest degree, charity or love must be directed toward another person.[7] Hilton describes this phenomenon even more exactly in saying that we do not actually "leave" God in loving our sisters and brothers: ". . . if you are wise you won't leave God but will find God and possess God and see God in your fellow-Christians as you do in prayer, but you will have God in another way."[8] For Hilton the greatness of the human person is measured by the degree to which one loves God and other human persons.[9] In conjunction with this model, contemporary feminist theology pushes us beyond the medieval context to recognize the implications of traditional conceptions of love of God and neighbor for our own time.

The Issue of Gender Language

Before embarking on a project which entails application of medieval themes to contemporary thought one of the first questions we must ask is how the image of God theme can be retrieved when it has been associated at times with the claim that man is truly and essentially the image of God, while woman is the image of God only derivatively and not even fully. Although we can find such explanations beginning even with scriptural passages,[10] such claims do not accurately represent the thought of the figures considered here. Because of space constraints I can do little more than mention this important topic, and state my own attempt to deal with it. I maintain that the inferiority of women is not built into the medieval theological system as a primary structural support, but rather appears as a form of gender symbolization carried over from the patriarchal society in which the authors lived.

Kari Borresen introduces two rubrics that are especially helpful for assessing medieval reflections on women: subordination and equivalence.[11] She isolates two dominant and conflicting attitudes in Augustine's and Aquinas' reflections on the nature and role of women. One she calls *subordination*, the view that woman is subordinate to man in the order of creation, or in the day-to-day existence of this world.[12] She calls the second dominant attitude *equivalence*, a term used to indicate the "identical value of man and woman as human persons."[13] The *imago Dei* theme arises here: ". . . equivalence according to the spirit of the Gospel belongs to the order of salvation, as the realization of the quality of divine image borne equally by man and woman."[14] Although the order of creation is androcentric, the order of salvation is theocentric, and thus, in the order of salvation, the woman "bound to her individual end, [finds] the complete fulfillment of herself as the image of God."[15]

The equivalence/subordination conflict is certainly present in the medieval authors we consider here. On the one hand they assert that all people are created in God's image; but, on the other, they at times distinguish between men and women on a secondary and nonessential level. Augustine, Richard and Walter's major source here, divides reason into superior and inferior reason: males symbolize superior reason and females inferior reason, just as the male/female relationship symbolizes the relationship between Christ and the Church. Significantly, however, he adds that

. . . although the physical and external differences of man and woman symbolize the double role that the mind is known to have in one man, nevertheless a woman, for all her physical qualities as *a woman, is actu-ally renewed in the spirit of her mind in the knowledge of God according to the image of her Creator, and therein there is no male or female* [my emphasis].[16]

Despite the symbolic female/male differences wherein woman represents the physical and man the spiritual, for the most part the medieval tradition affirmed that women and men are equally images of God. As this example indicates, we must read these medieval writers with a constant eye to patriarchal distortions, and to incon-sistencies in their claims about the human person. Although we should be always alert to the possibilities for systematic distortion, we need not summarily dismiss everything that has been said or written about male and female in these texts, particularly because they often include contradictory claims, that is, statements which disparage women because they are reflective of a patriarchal social context, and others which could be the basis for affirming the dignity and equality of all human beings, females and males.

Authors like Borresen, Eleanor McLaughlin,[17] and Caroline Walker Bynum[18] who perceive the conflict in medieval texts between equiva-lence and subordination, or between theocentric theory and andro-centric bias, have recognized that the medieval use of the *imago Dei* pushes writers at least in theory beyond what much medieval thought and practice taught concerning the subordinate status of women. The tensions and even contradictions in medieval comments about women suggest that the medieval world did not live out the full implications of the image theme. The equivalence signalled by the image of God tradition could have had significant implications not only in the order of salvation but also in the order of creation had its proponents admitted that affirmation of one's status as an image of God has significant implications for women and men in their rela-tions to one another and standing before God. The female and male equivalence signalled in the *imago Dei* theme refers to a practical, every-day perspective out of which we act in relation to God, self, and the world. In this way, we may be encouraged to reconsider this theme by Bynum's observation that "[I]f the images . . . have not in the societies that produced them brought about the equality of the sexes, it is not, so to speak, the fault of the image."[19] Symbols do not simply reflect dominant hierarchical societal values because they also carry with them the potential for radical social change and renewal.[20] Even when unrecognized by those using them, symbols, and specifically the image of God theme, "can invent as well as reinforce social values."[21]

In the context of Richard of St. Victor and Walter Hilton's thought I will ask here what the image of God concept meant, what potential it did express, and what emancipatory prospects it might offer for us today. In what follows I will attempt to draw together three central ideas associated with the *imago Dei* in medieval theology: the fundamental orientation of the human person to God, the dynamics of transformation in human existence, and the discourse of intimacy that defines the God/human nexus. I will offer three thesis statements about the image that reflect traditional and contemporary uses of the image theme.

I. Our Existence as Images of God Expresses Both a Capacity and a Present State. As We Develop as Images of God We Come to Express Our Full Humanity in a Unity of the "Thinking-Relational" Self, and We Learn to Respect the Image Character of Other Human Persons.

In the work of Richard of St. Victor and Walter Hilton the image of God in us describes both a state of being and a capacity. First, the image of God theme refers to a present, already-existing state of being in which we are defined in an originary way by our relationship to the Divine of whom we are reflections by nature. Presupposing the revelatory function of Scripture, the medieval tradition interprets Gen 1:26 to mean that human persons from their creation are constituted in an inalienable way as images of God. The narrative of the fall of Adam and Eve and the concomitant damaging of the image reflects the tradition's perception that the image is somehow blurred and not fully actualized in our experience, although the human person remains in a fundamental way, by virtue of its nature, an image of God.

Thus a second aspect of the image emerges: the image describes a capacity, namely that about us which makes it possible for us to grow in relationship with the Divine as the breach symbolized by the fall is healed. Although we may not yet fulfill our capacities, we are images of God already simply by virtue of the fact that we have the *ability* to know and to love, and to the extent that we actively love and know God we are developing as images and fulfilling our capacities in actuality. In referring to both an actuality and a potentiality the image alerts us to our nature and to our destiny. This is the logic of medieval anthropology: by virtue of our being images of God we are offered an intimate relationship to God, but it is only insofar as we are images of God that we are capable of receiving this heritage.

In the medieval tradition represented here the image concept guides and directs all aspects of the human person's relationship to the Divine. Growth in relationship to God is measured by one's *reformation* as an image of God. Writers like Walter Hilton describe the work of God and Christ in our lives as a process of reforming us in Christ's image. The image of God theme plays an integral role in the divine-human relationship: it is only insofar as we are image-bearers that we can even be rendered capable of the relationship, and our relationship to God is measured by the development of the image within us. Specifically, the image of God in us describes our capacity to become like God by understanding and loving the God who is love.

Rosemary Radford Ruether also employs the notion of capacity and present state in accepting the dichotomy of classical theology between a good creation represented by Christ and a fallen humanity which we primarily encounter now.[22] The *imago Dei*, "remanifest in history as Christ," represents authentic human nature, what we can be potentially—in other words, it represents a present human capacity.[23] For Ruether and for the image tradition explored here, though, there is no absolute dichotomy between *imago Dei* and fallen humanity (as there is, e.g., in Karl Barth). Our existence as images of God is more than simply a capacity since at times we experience the full or partial fulfillment of that capacity in our present state. As Ruether writes, "the fullness of redeemed humanity, as image of God, is something only partially disclosed under the conditions of history. We seek it as a future self and world, still not fully achieved, still not fully revealed. But we also discover it as our true self and world, the foundation of and ground of our being."[24] The image in us points to our nature and to our destiny.

Dorothee Soelle affirms some similar aspects of the *imago Dei* theme, although the concept plays no explicitly central role in her theological formulations. She associates the image theme with "the Jewish affirmation of our being created as images of God, empowered to grow into love and to become love ourselves."[25] "The directive is clear . . . We are beckoned to approximate God . . . Created in the image of God, we therefore are able to imitate God."[26] And what does the capacity refer to? In what does the imitation consist? For Soelle, representative of the political turn in contemporary theology, the fact that we are God's image-bearers means that our destiny is to realize God's justice in the world. Soelle draws here on Carter Heyward's understanding of God as power-in-relation which refers not to dominating power-over, but rather to the Divine's capacity to empower others to love,[27] and "to become love ourselves."[28] Insofar as we can become or are bearers of that love we are images of God in that we potentially are or actually become co-creators with the Divine. The challenge for feminist theology is to articulate recommendations for the implementation of justice in specific instances, but the Christian image of God tradition reminds us of our nature as having the capacity to fulfill God's way of being in the world and as actualizing our nature in doing so.

In calling for an end to the compartmentalizing of roles in our lives as one significant condition for attaining a justice which respects the full humanity of all persons, male and female, Ruether raises one of the issues the image of God theme can most productively address. She writes, "[W]omen want to integrate the public and the private, the political and the domestic spheres in a new relationship that allows the thinking-relational self to operate throughout human life as one integrated self, rather than fragmenting the psyche across a series of different social roles."[29] The image of God theme as described by Richard and Walter provides a theological concept which symbolizes exactly the holistic integration of the thinking-relational self Ruether advocates. The fact that we are image-bearers tells us that we are thinking-relational beings.

Both medieval thinkers identify a dual focus of the image, an identification with human understanding, often when they speak of knowledge of God, and with the human will, often when speaking of love of God. This dual focus is clarified in medieval attention to the constant interaction of knowledge and love, one encouraging the other. Knowledge of God for its own sake unrelated to love of God is useless, Hilton says;[30] or as Richard expresses it, love and knowledge work with one another and mutually encourage one another: "the richness of divine knowledge increases in vain, unless it increases the flame of divine love in us."[31] This is a theological reminder that our discussions of God are best rooted in a knowledge related to love; but, further, it is also a starting point for describing our relationship not only to God, but also to the world. Our two medieval theologians maintain that our relationship to God forms a model for our relationship to others and to the world around us. Love of neighbor, as described by the two Augustinian canons, is integrally related to love of God, and is so basic that we are by nature in-relation to God and in-relation to others at the same time. A knowledge in continual interplay with love, such as that described by Hilton and Richard, guides our development of rationality. Thus a theological anthropology dependent upon the medieval tradition would call for a constant interaction of knowledge and love in our relationship to other persons and to the world: we can see immediately the kind of implications this dialectic would have for a theological anthropology in exploring, for example, our relationship to our natural environment.

Our medieval theologians' vigilant reiteration of the constant interaction between knowledge and love cautions us to exercise care in using language like "thinking-relational" self, for such language used unreflectively can perpetuate the myth that there is a "thinking" self which can be clearly distinguished from the "relational" self. In actuality the two are not divisible in the manner such language would suggest.[32] All of our thinking is in some sense relational, and to the extent that it is not relational or is actively destructive of relationships it does not express full humanity. The separation of the two terms "thinking" and "relational" may have some limited use in making a distinction, such as Parker Palmer does, between a kind of knowledge which originates in curiosity or from control, and a knowledge arising from love or compassion.[33] Of course, even the first type of knowledge is relational – though the relational implications are negative in that they promote neither compassion nor respect for the dignity of all human persons. (Knowledge-based research for the Strategic Defense Initiative, for example, is not simply "pure knowledge." Potentially, it has tremendous relational consequences because it may, for example, actively contradict a 1971 Salt I agreement prohibiting development of Anti-Ballistic Missile Defense, thus undermining the emerging relationship described in the Salt I agreement.)

Traditionally many theologians have emphasized one or the other side of the love-knowledge dichotomy; indeed, theology in the second half of the twentieth-century can be characterized by its emphasis on love.[34] Perhaps, though, we need to reconsider for a moment the importance and possibilities for the theme of knowledge in the process of recognizing the full humanity of all human persons. We are taught to "love our neighbors," but this has little meaning; often, we cannot even determine who our neighbors are. The notion of "knowledge" could be helpful here. We would see things in a new way and in a way closer to the medieval insight if we were to imagine "knowing" our neighbors as images of God. Frequently we "know" people as "the sister or brother of so-and-so," "the husband or wife of so-and-so," "the author of a particular book," "the advocate of a particular cause." "Knowing someone as . . ." generally results in our having particular preconceived attitudes towards the person before ever meeting her or him. If we know someone as "an advocate of peace concerns," for example, we might expect (rightly or wrongly) the person to have particular interests or particular attitudes. How would we think differently if we were to "know" people as "images of God"?

Richard of St. Victor points us in this direction in making the insightful point that in spiritual matters we must love first by *deliberation*, and only later will we love by *affection*.[35] A first step of deliberation is a knowledge which we eventually come to understand more deeply and more experientially. We begin by emphasizing that we must first "know" ourselves and all other people as images of God, and after acting out of that knowledge, contemplating it, and striving to live from that perspective more faithfully, we then become able to love and understand more fully the meaning of our and all humanity's existence as images of God.

Contemporary theologians' attention to the political ramifications of our action in the world reiterates the medieval recognition of the emptiness that results from bifurcating love and knowledge. It is that very practice of dividing our lives into a series of separate and limited territories, separating the religious from the political, or the economic from the social, or the feminist from the theological, that makes it possible for us to talk about "love of neighbor" without making a commitment to economic sanctions, for example, which might free our neighbor from political, economic, or social oppression. In a variety of ways theologians like Ruether and Soelle affirm the interconnectedness of our lives and focus especially on the too-often-neglected political nature of theology. In their explicit attention to political matters their starting point and central concerns differ from those of Richard of St. Victor or Walter Hilton and their emphases shed new light on the implications of the image of God theme; however, the basis for using the image tradition to speak of each and every person's originary constitution and dignity as a reflection of the Divine and use of the image concept to highlight the interrelationship between love and knowledge can be traced back to the medieval insights examined here.

II. The Way to Image Restoration Is By Way of Spiritual Transformation, Including the Cultivation of Self-Knowledge, the Active Metamorphosis of Vices into Virtues, and the Pursuit of Love and Knowledge of God.

As we have seen in the cases of Richard of St. Victor and Walter Hilton, in medieval thought the image theme often appears in the context of holistic descriptions of a Christian life of seeking to imitate God by "becom[ing] love and not just receiv[ing] it."[36] The image of God theme and its medieval articulation highlights the transformative nature of human persons. Practical and moral analyses of the image consistently chart the dynamics of this transformative process through which persons seek to actualize their potential as bearers of the Divine image. While the specific stages of transformation are articulated in different ways, the development is frequently depicted as a journey, variously described as a process of faith seeking understanding, or as a process of the transformation of the image of sin within us into an image of Jesus.

While I am not advocating a wholesale return to medieval categories of transformation, I do want to point to the critical role accorded transformation in medieval understandings of the human person, and most visibly in medieval discussions of the image of God theme. Although as theologians we sustain ourselves by hope for transformation in the world around us we too often focus on the way things should be, or on the way things are, with little regard for cultivating the process of effecting change. Guided by medieval descriptions of the transformative process we might renew our vigor in attending to the place of change in human existence.

Almost without exception medieval portrayals of development as images of God begin with the pursuit of self-knowledge, a lengthy process attainable only with the help of grace. Self-knowledge leads people to recognize two things (1) that we are image-bearers, and therein lies our dignity (and the source for unwavering self-love); and (2) that we frequently neglect our responsibilities and capacities as image-bearers. In spite of the medieval spiritual theology's undeserved reputation for focusing on sin in believers' lives, the fundamental affirmation underlying the texts considered here is that humanity is good and directed toward growth and transformation. Self-knowledge, cultivated with attention to the disparity between what we are (blurred images) and what we can be (clear images), leads both to a restoration of a good will and to a knowledge gained through experience of what we may know already by faith or by the teaching of Christian communities. Self-knowledge seeks knowledge and love of God; it "assum[es] . . . another relationship to reality, one of wholeness."[37]

Most of us at times experience disjunction or disunity, a sense of alienation from the world around us and from God. We could argue as Hilton does that our enslavement to vices such as apathy, gluttony, pride, and lechery, accounts for our disjunction with the world.[38] And we could argue that progress in the transformation of vices into virtues signals progress in growth as images of God so that the virtues he prescribes as correctives to vice are useful to characterize the situation in which we would be at one with the world.

There are, however, some other contemporary ways to convey the sense of what Hilton suggested with his contrast between vices, or sin, and virtues.

Like many contemporary theologians, Ruether understands sin in part as a distortion of our relationships to others and to the world around us; in particular, it is a "distortion of the self-other relationship into the good-evil, superior-inferior dualism."[39] Sexism is a primary example of sin since sexism presumes and perpetuates distorted, bifurcated relationality.[40] Sin refers not only to our active participation in relationships dominated by pride, but also to "the passivity of men and women who acquiesce to the group ego."[41] The process of developing self-knowledge can help counter situations of distorted relationality by encouraging us to recognize our own capacities to oppress others, to promote a sexist status quo, and to close our eyes to injustice.[42]

Dorothee Soelle is even more sensitive to the significance of spiritual development and more vocal about the political and social demands of Christianity than Ruether. She deepens the understanding of our distorted relationality to the world by naming its five characteristics: (1) isolation, (2) reduction to the individual, (3) muteness and speechlessness, (4) fatalism and apathy, and (5) immanence.[43] What is the antidote to this situation? The tradition has answered "Virtue," and writers such as Richard of St. Victor have called love the chief of all virtues. But how do we understand "virtues" and "love" today? Soelle names an antidote to each of the vices named above and the common denominator of all the "virtues" is solidarity, the cultivation of full humanity, an active recognition of the uniqueness, value, and interconnectedness of each human being and of all human beings. Her catalogue of contemporary "virtues" vis-à-vis the "vices" of modernity are the following: (1) connectedness, (2) collective experience, (3) symbolic and linguistic expression, (4) readiness for political action, and (5) transcendence.

Connectedness is the opposite of isolation because in affirming our connectedness we affirm our solidarity, our interdependence. Rather than celebrating the individuality of our experience we appreciate its collective nature. Affirming our own and others' experiences, and struggling to find a voice to express them, we deny fatalism and we emerge from the pit of apathy. As we demand our right to speak and the rights of others to speak we enter into the political arena to assure voices for collective human experience. Listening to others and speaking to others calls for transcendence, an ability to look beyond

our immediate surroundings to a future, to the practical consequences of what we do and say.

Although Soelle does not pose the question in quite this way, it is
important to ask how we move from the situation of seclusion to the
situation of solidarity. More implicit than explicit, but present in
Soelle's work seems to be the claim that the inward journey, the
spiritual path, provides the means for moving from seclusion to
solidarity. The "way of inwardness" has love (here understood as
solidarity) as its goal and involves a process of development, which
can be understood in terms of a movement from the negative side to
the positive side of the polarities she describes.

> The most important virtue of this kind of relation is not obedience but
> solidarity, for solidarity asks that we change the image of God from that
> of a power-dispensing father to one of a liberating and unifying force,
> that we cease to be objects and become subjects involved in this process
> of change, that we learn cooperation rather than wait for things to come
> to us from on high.[44]

Soelle advocates the inward journey as the way to learn to experience a new and deeper unifying love, or solidarity. As with Richard
and Walter we begin with the affirmation that "God is Love" which
for Soelle we recognize in particular historical experiences of liberation. The tendency of God's love, which becomes present to us in the
experience of solidarity,[45] is to increase, to grow, "to bind and join
together in even larger entities."[46] The image of God is reformed in
us to the extent that we are capable of participating in God's active
and ever-widening love. But it is not an easy process because we are
accustomed to avoiding pain; we are used to narrowing our vision to
protect our own private stability and comfort.[47] Soelle, and the
tradition represented by Richard of St. Victor and Walter Hilton,
challenges us to trade security and control for a life which includes
publicly "seeking God." Richard says we love first by deliberation in
spiritual things as the soul turns inward and pursues self-knowledge
through cultivation of virtues and intentions. At some stage of the
process, after the initial steps of reordering one's priorities and seeking to act out of love and understanding in the world, many medieval
spiritual theologians describe an aspect of transformative experience
which focuses almost exclusively on the Divine, culminating in a
union with God, interpreted by Richard of St. Victor and Walter
Hilton as a union of wills. Significantly, though, in the moral and
practical image tradition represented here, the process of image
reformation does not end until finally, we "go forth because of our

neighbor."[48] Soelle writes, "[t]he goal . . . is to reach this farthest point, to experience the deepest self-conformation, and yet to return and to communicate the experience that we are a part of the whole."[49]

III. The Goal of Image Restoration Is the Conformity of Our Wills to God's Will So That One Perceives Oneself Not as a Servant of the Divine, But Rather as a Friend of God.

Christ plays a central role in medieval depictions of persons' response to God's offer of love in that, as Hilton explains, we begin the transformation process by contemplating Christ's humanity, by cultivating our resemblance to Jesus. Richard echoes this when he says that " . . . one who does not follow the footsteps of Christ perfectly does not enter the way of truth rightly."[50] He describes the highest earthly stage of love of God in terms of conformity of our wills to the image of Christ: "In this state the image of the will of Christ is set before the soul so that these words come to her: 'Let this mind be in you, which was also in Christ Jesus.'"[51] Dorothee Soelle uses the same passage from Phil 2:5 "to have this mind . . . which you have in Christ Jesus." She explicates it in a similar way to Richard: "Living as Christ lived means the inward journey to . . . surrendering of the ego and the return journey to the midst of the world."[52] Richard makes the point that in this fourth degree we are torn between being "dissolved and being with Christ" and remaining in the flesh which the "charity of Christ compels."[53] His contrast captures the experience of the person who, having tasted the love of God, on the one hand, longs to be taken up completely into that love to dwell entirely within it, but who, on the other hand, cognizant of humanity's existence as an embodied reality, recognizes the significance of loving others in concrete experience as an expression of our love of God. Charity compels us to go out into the world with compassion.

This discussion of conformity of wills to Christ raises the problematic issue of contemporary appropriations, and in particular, feminist appropriations of Christ. Although I have no satisfactory Christological formulation to offer, I think it is important to acknowledge that we can no longer simply issue a call to imitate Christ without considering the implications of Christ's existence as a *male* human person.[54] At this point, I, like Ruether in *Sexism and God-talk,* focus on Christ's work as a renewer of the Word of God who "does not validate the existing social and religious hierarchy but speaks on behalf of the marginalized and despised groups of society,"[55] and I affirm, as have many influenced by issues of sexism and patriarchy, that "[t]heologically speaking . . . the maleness of Christ has no ultimate significance." I am well aware, though, that in Christian ecclesiastical traditions the maleness of Christ has at times been regarded as having importance, and even ultimate significance for some theologies of ministry. The consequences of this way of thinking are clear in the Roman Catholic use of Christ's "maleness" to claim that only men have the capacity to be priests. Image of Christ language is drawn into the discussion and is used here to subordinate women: "the priest, who alone has the power to perform it [celebration of the Eucharist], then acts not only through the effective power conferred on him by Christ, but *in persona Christi*, taking the role of Christ, to the point of being his very image, when he pronounces the words of consecration."[57] The implication is that Christ's maleness has a certain ultimate significance: "The incarnation of the Word took place according to the male sex: this is indeed a question of fact, and this fact, while not implying an alleged natural superiority of man over woman, cannot be disassociated from the economy of salvation. . . ."[58]

The role of the maleness of Christ quickly becomes an issue in a retrieval of the *imago Dei*, since Christ was regarded as *the* Image of God and insofar as we learn to love and understand Christ as human and divine we learn to love and understand God. In speaking of Christ as both human and divine the western Christian tradition sought to indicate at the very least that Christ presented God to the world in a particularly vivid way. And perhaps this is the very least Christians can say now, namely that Christ's life and way of being in the world leads us to understand and to love God. For the time being we can affirm what Ruether and Soelle do as very similar to the insights of Walter Hilton: we can say that imitation of Christ leads to a moral shift which will in time change our way of being in the world. This moral shift will disallow the patriarchal focus on the maleness of Jesus and promote instead the full humanity and gender-inclusive message and mission of the saving Christ. It will in no way deny the particularities of Jesus' ethnic and sexual identity, but it will not use these particularities to undermine the complete participation of all people – male and female – in the religious, social, and political dimensions of human existence.

The discourse of intimacy used to describe the relationship between image-bearers and the Divine vividly conveys the nature of the practical and operational shift that results from allying oneself with Christ's way of being in the world. Far from construing the lot of image-bearers as being one of mere obedience to a dictatorial exemplar whom we mechanically imitate from a great distance,[59] the dominant imagery expressing our relationship to God as images is language of friendship and even marriage.

Citing Scripture to characterize the intimacy between God and persons who have pursued actualization of their capacities as image-bearers, Richard writes: "Do you wish to know that the loftiness of divine showings may be an open disclosure of divine love? 'Now I do not call you servants but friends,' [Christ] says. . . . "[60] This relationship to the Divine suggests a model for our relationships to others, and provides opposition to "Christian" relationships of domination and oppression. Indeed, servant-language is to be fully replaced by friendship discourse and language of dialogue in which persons take God's way of being as their own in carrying on their work in the world. Hilton evokes spousal or lover imagery in describing Scripture as love letters to the human person: "You may be very sure that all such grace-giving knowledge, in Holy Scriptures or within any other writing that is made through grace, is nothing else but love letters and messages exchanged between a loving soul and Jesus the Beloved."[61]

In considering the image of God tradition feminist thought can acknowledge and retrieve traditional alternatives to relating to God as the "Almighty Father."[62] The Christian image tradition, starting with the affirmation that we are images of God, signals our closeness to God through speaking of the union of wills with the Divine and by invoking language of intimacy. The focus in traditional interpretations of the *imago Dei* theme is on our nearness to God and on the possibilities for advancing that nearness to the point where we may be considered friends of God.

Conclusion

This discussion set out to illustrate some of the preliminary points of convergence between medieval reflections on the image of God theme and contemporary reflections on the human person, suggesting that feminist theology can reclaim this image of God tradition as a resource which describes a holistic and responsible way of life, and encouraging further consideration of this and other symbols that have potential for affirming the full humanity of all persons, female and male.

The image of God theme is a concept that conveys something of our relationship to God, self, and the world. We move from the datum of revelation that we are created in God's image to the process of actively realizing our potential as images of God by cultivating the unity of the "thinking-relational self," and by learning to see and actively respond to others as images of God (a response which includes political, economic and social action). We seek to become images of God by becoming images of Christ by way of a conformity of will, that is, by directing ourselves to the community around us in charity and understanding. We look inward, actively cultivate our relationship to God, and, as Richard said, we "go out into the world in compassion"[63] to affirm the full humanity of all people as images of God.

Feminist theology, as a significant voice in contemporary theological reflection, can affirm the tradition's recognition that all people are created in God's image. It can further draw on the tradition's insight that while the image points to a present state of all created human persons it points also to a relational capacity of all human persons to actualize their abilities to love and to know the Divine and the world around them. While theologians like Ruether and Soelle recognize the features of distorted and healthy relationality, we might be even more attentive to the tradition's insight concerning the importance of transformation as a basic experience of the human person in the world. By placing the medieval and contemporary traditions into dialogue with one another, we become reflective about the nature of the transformative process as a way to guide human persons to fulfillment of their capacities to love and to know.

Despite its sometimes checkered history with respect to speaking about the full humanity of women, the vision of the God/human/world relationship described in the image of God tradition may offer support for feminist theology's retrieving imagery from the Christian tradition. The image of God tradition does not lead believers to a slavish imitation of a domineering God; rather the God of whom we are images appears as a friend, and even as a spouse, inviting all of us to share in the creative and emancipatory work of love and understanding in the world.

NOTES

1. I would like to thank Mark Wallace for his helpful comments on this article, Bernard McGinn for reading this at an earlier stage, and my colleagues in Soundings at Boston College for their conversation about this material.

2. The Latin *imago Dei* makes this clear.

3. E.g., 1 Cor 11:7.

4. A second tendency, represented by thinkers like Nemesius of Emesa (4th c.) and John the Scot (9th c.), is to focus on the metaphysical dimensions of the image.

5. Rosemary Radford Ruether, *Sexism and God-talk* (Boston: Beacon Press, 1983) 113.

6. "We are living parts of active love" [Dorothee Soelle with Shirley A. Cloyes, *To Work and to Love: A Theology of Creation* (Philadelphia: Fortress Press, 1984) 43].

7. References are given to *The Twelve Patriarchs*, (hereafter *TP*), The Mystical Ark (*MA*), and Book Three of the Trinity (*DT*) by book (where applicable), chapter, page reference in Patrologia Latina for *TP* and *MA*, and for *DT* to book, chapter, and page number in Jean Ribaillier's (*R*) critical edition of *De Trinitate* (Paris: J. Vrin, 1958). This reference is to Grover Zinn, trans., *Richard of St. Victor: The Twelve Patriarchs, The Mystical Ark, Book Three of the Trinity* (New York: Paulist Press, 1979) *DT*, 3:2:374; R, 3.2: 136. (Since all *Patrologia Latina* references to Richard of St. Victor are from Volume 196, I include here column number only).

8. The *Stairway of Perfection* will be referred to in the notes as *SP*; references are to book, chapter, and page reference in the English translation. The reference is to Walter Hilton, *The Stairway of Perfection*, trans. M. L. Del Mastro (New York: Image Books, 1979) 1.83; 175–176.

9. Hilton says, "As much as you know and love God and your fellow-Christians, so great is your soul" (*ibid., SP*, 1.89; 182).

10. 1 Cor 11:7.

11. Kari Borreson, *Subordination and Equivalence: The Nature and Role of Women in Augustine and Thomas Aquinas* (Washington, D.C.: University Press of America, 1981).

12. *Ibid.* xvii.

13. *Ibid.*

14. *Ibid.*

15. *Ibid.* 335.

16. Augustine, *The Literal Meaning of Genesis*, trans. John Hammond Taylor (New York: Newman Press, 1982) 3.22.34; 99. It may be helpful to see the original here: cf. *De Genesi ad litteram* in Augustine, *Opera Omnia*, ed. Benedictine Monks of S. Maur (Paris: Gaume Fratres, 1836) vol. 3; 263D, *Itaque quamvis hoc in duobus hominibus diversi sexus exterius secundum corpus figuratum sit, quod etiam in una hominis interius mente intelligitur; tamen et femina quae est corpore femina, renovatur etiam ipsa in spiritu mentis suae in agnitione Dei secundum imaginem ejus qui creavit, ubi non est masculus et femina.*

17. Eleanor McLaughlin, "Equality of Souls, Inequality of Sexes: Woman in Medieval Theology," in *Religion and Sexism: Images of Woman in the Jewish and Christian Traditions*, ed. Rosemary Radford Ruether (New York: Simon and Schuster, 1974) 213–266.

18. Caroline Walker Bynum, "'And Woman His Humanity': Female Imagery in the Religious Writing of the Later Middle Ages," in *Gender and Religion: On the Complexity of Symbols*, Caroline Walker Bynum, Stevan Harell, and Paula Richman, eds. (Boston: Beacon Press, 1986) 257–288.

19. Caroline Walker Bynum, "Introduction: The Complexity of Symbols," in *Gender and Religion* 8.

20. Symbols also have power as "inventing, questioning, rejecting and transcending gender as it is constructed in the individual's psychological development and sociological setting" (*ibid.*).

21. *Ibid.*, 15.

22. Ruether, *Sexism and God-talk* 38.

23. *Ibid.* 93.

24. *Ibid.* 114.

25. Soelle, *To Work and to Love* 43.

26. *Ibid.* 42.

27. "When will you discover that all is possible to her who participates in God's power?" (*ibid.*, 46).

28. *Ibid.*, 43.

29. Ruether, *Sexism and God-talk* 113.

30. Hilton, *SP*, 2.34;289.

31. Richard of St. Victor, *MA*, 4:10;274, 145C-D.

32. For an excellent analysis of this see Mary Midgley, *Beast and Man: The Roots of Human Nature* (Ithaca, N.Y.: Cornell University Press, 1978).

33. Parker J. Palmer, *To Know as We Are Known: A Spirituality of Education* (San Francisco: Harper and Row, n.d.) 8.

34. See, e.g., Jürgen Moltmann, Karl Rahner, Thomas Merton, Dorothee Soelle.

35. Richard of St. Victor, *MA*, 4.11:274; 146A.

36. Dorothee Soelle, *Death By Bread Alone: Texts and Reflections on Religious Experience*, trans. David L. Scheidt (Philadelphia: Fortress Press, 1975) 102.

37. *Ibid.* 79.

38. Hilton, *SP*, 1.78;170

39. Ruether, *Sexism and God-talk* 163.

40. *Ibid.* 174.

41. *Ibid.* 164.

42. *Ibid.* 188.

43. Dorothee Soelle, *The Strength of the Weak: Towards a Christian Feminist Identity*, trans. Robert and Rita Kimber (Philadelphia: Westminster Press, 1984) 11-22.

44. *Ibid.* 103.

45. Idem, *Death By Bread Alone* 134.

46. *Ibid.* 137.

47. *Ibid.* 9.

48. References to Richard of St. Victor's *De quatuor quadibus violentae caritatis* given to page numbers in Claire Kirchberger's English translation and to

Gervais Dumiege's critical Latin edition. This reference is to Richard of St. Victor *Dq*, 224; *D*, 29:157.

49. Soelle, *Death By Bread Alone* 69.

50. Richard of St. Victor, *TP*, 79:136; 56C-D.

51. *Ibid.*, *Dq*, 230; *D*, 43:171.

52. Soelle, *Death By Bread Alone* 135.

53. *Ibid.*, *Dq*, 230; *D*, 44:173.

54. For discussion of these issues see: Anne Marie Gardiner, ed., *Women and Catholic Priesthood: An Expanded Vision* (New York: Paulist Press, 1976); Leon Swidler and Arlene Swidler, eds., *Women Priests: A Catholic Commentary on the Vatican Declaration* (New York: Paulist Press, 1977).

55. Ruether, *Sexism and God-talk* 136.

56. *Ibid.* 137.

57. Swidler, *Women Priests* 26 (Sacred Congregation for the Doctrine of the Faith, "Declaration on the Question of the Admission of Women to the Ministerial Priesthood," 5.26).

58. *Ibid.* 5.28.

59. Another productive area of dialogue between medieval and contemporary theology is in the area of imitation. In this regard see Karl Morrison, *The Mimetic Tradition of Reform in the West* (Princeton: Princeton University Press, 1982).

60. Richard of St. Victor, *MA*, 4.16:288; 155B.

61. Hilton, *SP*, 2.43;332. Or, again, "The lover of Jesus is his friend, not because he desires it, but because God, of His merciful goodness makes him His friend by a true agreement. And therefore, He shows His secrets to him, as to a true friend who pleases Him with love (rather than one who serves Him through fear, like a slave)" (*ibid.* 2.43; 329).

62. A recent excellent example of this which might make even more explicit links to the Christian tradition is Sallie McFague's *Models of God: Theology for an Ecological, Nuclear Age* (Philadelphia: Fortress Press, 1987).

63. Richard of St. Victor, *Dq*, 224; *D*, 29:157.

"The Devils Are Come Down Upon Us": Myth, History and the Witch as Scapegoat

MARTHA REINEKE
University of Northern Iowa

> If our ancestors had thought in the same mode as do today's masters, they would never have put an end to the witch trials.
>
> René Girard[1]

How do I examine women's history as a feminist? In a recent article, Adrienne Rich reminds us that history is more than tales of our finest hours. History is forged in a struggle for consciousness waged against the forces of amnesia. Rich tells us that, when a feminist breaks silence with history, she does more than invoke women from the past, for feminist history is history "charged with meaning." Charged by history to know the past in order to make choices for the future, each feminist is asked also to recover the lost memories of women, but only in ways that do not perpetuate the structures of history-making that first relegated women to invisibility.[2] Rich's words echo those of Phyllis Trible who suggests that a feminist "interprets stories of outrage on behalf of their female victims in order to recover a neglected history, to remember a past that the present embodies, and to pray that these terrors shall not come to pass again. In telling sad stories, a feminist seeks to redeem the time."[3] She recounts the past *in memoriam*.

In this essay, my own efforts to take the charge of history to heart focus on the witch hunts, 1450–1750. Notwithstanding recent scholarly efforts to redress Reformation historians' prior neglect of the witch hunts, I want to claim that current analyses, attentive as they are to tracing the demographic, economic, and sociological factors of the witch hunts in evermore sophisticated ways, are inadequate to the goals of feminist scholarship. My complaint focuses on the portrait of an extrinsic relation of religion to witch hunting offered by most recent scholarship and on the scholarly treatment of the violence that attended witch hunting. The people who accused women of witchcraft, who put them on trial, tortured, banished, or executed them, explained their reasons by appeal to religious beliefs, but those beliefs, according to many current theories, were but external trappings for other social, political, and economic agendas. Chosen for its efficacy and by historical accident, religion accompanied the witch hunts but did not form or define them. Moreover, while wisely avoiding a detailed analysis of the violence that attended the witch hunts which might verge on voyeurism, current scholarship has met their violence with virtual silence. Neither the torture of the accused nor the violent deaths of the convicted have been explained adequately. Because these analyses of witch hunting bypass the issue of the intrinsic relation of religion to those hunts and do not engage in a systematic attention to the violence of those hunts, they are seriously flawed. Specifically, because they misread the dynamics of persecution, these analyses leave the persecutors unchallenged, perpetuating the victimization of the women charged and convicted by those persecutors. Despite their attention to detail and evidence, current scholarly analyses share an amnesia which I now believe we ignore at our peril.

The issue of amnesia is particularly acute for feminist scholars of religion who study the witch craze. Lest we become forgetful of the diverse resources that found our work and utilize only a narrow range of disciplinary perspectives, I offer this essay as a cautionary tale to those who find themselves, as I have found myself, captivated by current trends in witch craze scholarship. Our attraction is understandable: in the interests of identifying with women accused of witchcraft and making their victimization visible, we are wary of explanations that might mute these women's voices further. On behalf of the victims of the witch hunts, we distance ourselves from the voices of their accusers, for we fear that if we make reflections on the accusers' mythic discourse of demonology the linchpin of our analyses, we risk offering accounts of the craze that overlook the victims. Reducing the range of our inquiry, we do not extend an appreciation for myth, prominent in much of our work, to our reflections on Reformation demonology. Not surprisingly, we then make common cause with those social scientists who, in dismissing demonology or "translating" it in terms of a political ideology, also seem to give voice to the victims of witch hunting by silencing their accusers.

I will argue that, when feminist scholars in religious studies engage in selective inquiries about the witch craze that bypass mythic discourse, we seriously underestimate the resources of our discipline at a point where they are most crucial for our work *in memoriam* on behalf of our foresisters. To speak adequately of the witch craze, to remember all that we must remember if we are to free our foresisters from a history of victimization, we must treat myth as essential to the witch craze and its violence.

In order to establish my argument I will summarize current theories of the witch craze. Then, appealing to the work of René Girard, I will challenge the adequacy of these scholarly explanations and point to a need to refocus current strategies of analysis in order to be more responsive to the charge of feminist history.

The Witch in Historical Perspective

Over three hundred years that span 1450 to 1750, women throughout Europe and in the American colonies were accused of witchcraft, tried, convicted, and executed.[4] Witches—persons who practiced magical arts, sorcery, and healing—had always been part of the European cultural landscape, but it was not until the fifteenth century that prosecution of them began to reach panic proportions. Prior to that time, legal charges were brought against individuals only if their sorcery caused personal or property damages. Recent scholarship cites a variety of factors that contributed to the development of a witch craze. These factors locate women accused of witchcraft at points of flux in the society where changes in the legal system, in marriage patterns, in the economy, and in the dominant social ethic and gender ideology were most dramatic and unsettling.

Christina Larner cites a changed legal system as an essential precondition of the witch craze. Interpersonal, restorative justice was in transition in the sixteenth century to a system of retributive justice. Where formerly an individual took the initiative to bring charges of sorcery against a neighbor who had harmed him or his family and also assumed the risk of reverse charges should the case be proved frivolous or unsound, now centralized systems came into existence which functioned on the premise that the whole society was the potential victim of witchcraft. For example, in Scotland, statutes against witchcraft, formerly linked with sexual and religious offenses, were abstracted from their traditional ecclesiastical context. The Scottish Witchcraft Act of 1563, like that of the Holy Roman Empire in 1532 (*Constitutio Criminalis Carolina*), made witchcraft a civil offense.[5] As centralized and secularized processes of control replaced the mode of individual prosecution of neighbor against neighbor, religious beliefs functioned in service to a secular system.

According to Erik Midelfort, preconditions for the witch craze in southwestern Germany during the latter half of the sixteenth century were founded similarly in a new legal possibility: the inquisitorial trial.[6] Traditional functions of an accuser were taken over by the court. A single panel included as one body the accuser, the prosecutor, and the judge. The skill of the examiners resulted in increasing numbers of charges, trials, and convictions.[7] Only two items of proof were needed to find a person guilty. First, three independent denunciations had to be offered. Under torture, women were called to denounce other women. Since the denunciations had to be made independently, that three different persons would name the same suspects tended to limit suspects to two groups: women notorious in the community for eccentric or unusual behavior or well-known women (e.g., midwives, wives of village innkeepers or well-known merchants).[8] The second item of proof was a devil's mark, a sign of one's relationship to the devil. A devil's mark was any spot on the body that was insensitive to pricking with a pin or needle or which failed to bleed if pricked. Women suspected of witchcraft were stripped and searched for devil's marks. In some areas of Europe, professional prickers made an occupation of the search for these marks.[9] This new legal system set in motion a remarkably efficient machinery for witch hunting.

Why did witch hunters, in utilizing this new legal system, find their victims almost exclusively among women?[10] Midelfort offers two explanations. First, women were believed to be prone to the devil's seduction. They were both more lustful and weaker than men. Thus, women as a group were vulnerable to the suspicions of witchcraft.[11] Second, a change in marriage patterns in the sixteenth century created widespread social instability and uncertainty. An excess of women of marriageable age, a high number of spinsters and widows, and a late age for marriage increased women's vulnerability in a society beset by social unrest.[12]

The specific rationale for the late marriage pattern is traced to the high standard of living in Western Europe. Late marriage brought about wealth, because one could conserve resources over many years; wealth, or the insistence on it, brought about late marriage. The standard of wealth was property, and in the sixteenth century men had to wait for land to become available, generally until their father's deaths. The stem-family pattern, according to which the eldest son inherited his father's property, contributed to the economic incentive for late marriage.[13]

The changed marriage pattern threatened patriarchal control and caused a fundamental disturbance in the family unit.[14] When efforts were made to consolidate patriarchal control, unmarried women were viewed increasingly with suspicion. Moreover, on a practical level, unmarried women were outside the key institution—the family—that would offer them protection. Widows and spinsters number high among the initial victims of witchcraft charges. Once in court, the sophisticated process of condemnation, founded on the principle of three independent denunciations, would extend as well to less-suspect members of the society.

For Carol Karlsen, historian of the witch hunts in New England, that women accused of witchcraft were women who threatened the economic order is of decisive significance. Daughters of families without sons, mothers of only female children, and women with no children predominated among the women charged with witchcraft. Women in these categories "were aberrations in an inheritance system designed to keep property in the hands of men."[15] In New England, women without male heirs comprised sixty-four percent of the females prosecuted for witchcraft, seventy-six percent of those found guilty, and eighty-nine percent of those executed.[16]

Like Midelfort, Karlsen traces tension in the social order to the intersection of familial and economic pressures. The new European marriage pattern occurred in New England in the late seventeenth century. Moreover, at that late date, changes in the family unit coincided with disruptions associated with the society's transition from a landbased to a mercantile economy. Sons who wanted their inheritance, but faced a shortage of land, experienced frustration and resentment. So also did the religious and landed elites and a newly risen, religiously diverse mercantile elite who competed with each other. Because the basic economic unit in the late seventeenth century was the family, to whom one owed respect, not complaints, and because there were few institutional avenues available to all alike to deal with economic conflict, witch hunting, Karlsen argues, became the vehicle of stress release. That frustration and resentment was then visited on the witch who, in Puritan belief, had come to symbolize all that was disorderly and evil in the society. The Salem witch trials were the clearest indication that in an economic war, competitors vied for control by using women as pawns in their struggle. Accusers tended to come from the old farm economy and those accused of witchcraft from the new mercantile economy that was threatening the old order.[17]

In addition to familial and economic disruptions to the social order, insecurities about social mores contributed to a climate of suspicion conducive to witch hunting. Villages and developing towns throughout Europe were experiencing a transition from a communal ethic to an ethic of individualism: a tradition of mutual help was being challenged by a new economic order.[18] That change exacted its highest cost from those persons who had depended most on the older order of charity: widows, the poor, the elderly. In transition from old to new ethic, residents of a community were more likely to resent a neighbor's appeal for help, yet to feel guilty about their refusal of help. Notably, the accuser in the witch trial was nearly always more prosperous than the accused. Moreover, the poorest of the poor generally escaped charges of witchcraft. Instead, the border-line case—the moderately-poor woman who felt she ought to receive her neighor's help but whose overtures were rejected—was most likely to be linked to witchcraft.[19] With the decline of a social ethic, which had been firmly articulated by the church in previous times, the individual bore sole responsibility for adjudicating the parameters of charity. Not until the state, in the next century, made charity the province of a government bureaucracy would a social ethic be articulated clearly again. In the transition period, the guilt feelings of an individual uncertain about his or her responsibility to a neighbor became "fertile ground" for witchcraft accusations. Misfortunes might be a witch's retaliation against her neighbor.[20]

John Demos argues that this scenario is particularly applicable to witch hunting among the Puritans in New England. Although the Puritans brought with them to the New World the traditional ethic of Christian charity, court records of struggles over land, money, and inheritances demonstrate that these fragile communities were fed increasingly on an ethic of individualism. Marginalized women, at greater risk in communities populated by people maneuvering for "personal advantage," bore the brunt of communal insecurity about the new ways.[21]

Insecurity about new social mores characterizes another factor contributing to the witch hunts: new gender ideologies offered by the Church created unrest similar to that unrest associated with the new ethic of individualism. Both Karlsen and Larner note the ambiguous status of women during the sixteenth and seventeenth centuries in respect to expectations for their gender. On the one hand, the pre-Reformation view that women, morally inferior to men, were weak-willed and susceptible both to lusts of the flesh and to enticements to greed, still functioned. On the other hand, and more explicitly, voices of the Reformation espoused a new gender ideology: women, granted a greater autonomy and capacity for virtuous behavior, were responsible for the state of their souls.[22] These twin religious ideologies of gender, appropriated by the state, had major consequences in women's lives. On the basis of the *pre-Reformation* theology that still formed the background to cultural perceptions of women, the witch hunters could justify a position that made witch hunting synonymous with woman hunting. On the basis of *Reformation* theology, the witch hunters could make women responsible, as pre-Reformation governments had not, for the crime of witchcraft.

Prior to the Scottish Witchcraft Act, women were invisible in the courts. Their behavior was the responsibility of their husbands and fathers and the punishment for any crimes they had committed was that thought appropriate for children, whipping.[23] With the Witchcraft Act in force, the state began to explore the parameters of women's responsibility for their own behavior.

Indeed, Larner argues that the contrasting theologies of gender were introduced into the court in order for the state to educate women to their new roles.[24] Women who misjudged the limits of their responsibility and saw a license for equality in the Reformation's affirmation of their capacity for responsible behavior were instructed by the witch trials to the error of their views. The witchcraft trials were therefore pedagogical: by means of the trials, lines of appropriate female behavior were drawn, and overly independent women had the new theory of female responsibility turned back on themselves.

Karlsen's study of accusations of witchcraft directed against radical Puritan women, such as Ann Hutchinson and Mary Dyer, who believed that the mandate for spiritual equality before God justified equality in the church, closely parallels Larner's. Basing their views on the notion that gender arrangements were not only divinely ordained by God but mandated by nature, the Puritan male leadership strove to disabuse women such as Hutchinson and Dyer of their views.[25] That women accused of witchcraft were linked with the crimes of bearing illegitimate children, having abortions, or committing infanticide[26] served to confirm, for that leadership, witches'

sinful interference with divinely ordained gender roles. So also did
imagery associated with witches—they hatched, bred, or suckled
either heretical ideas and/or actual monsters—exemplify the Puritan
male leadership's view of witches' sinful challenge of divine mandate.[27] Unmarried women, childless women, midwives, and women
in business—all aberrations in the divinely ordained system that
defined women by their role in procreation—were particularly vulnerable to charges of witchcraft.

Again, like Larner, Karlsen traces the preoccupation with gender
roles in colonial New England to the ambiguity of those roles in
Puritan society. As was the case in Scotland, Puritan views of gender
maintained an implicit reference to the pre-Reformation suspicions
about women while externally advocating a more optimistic portrait
of women. Karlsen argues that the witch trials ensued during the
time in which both views were still held. The trials were, in some
ways, the very occasion for adjudicating the truth about women.[28]
The witch was the negative model by which the virtuous Puritan
woman was defined. She set off in stark relief the values of Puritan
society and the borders of its moral and cultural universe.[29]

The Witch as Scapegoat

For each scholar of the witch hunts, contributing factors, such as
those discussed above, form the background for analyses of essential
aspects of the craze. The figure of the scapegoat appears in three
typologies that frame the witch craze: the witch as scapegoat served
the ideological interests of the ruling-class, or she was chosen to bear
the brunt of the fears of the peasant class, or, standing at the juncture
of popular and learned cultures, needed by each, she was the one
torn apart in their struggles with each other. For none of these
typologies was religious belief—myth and practice—central to the
witch craze. Religious discourse was located at the periphery; other
factors constituted the core dynamic of witch hunting.

Erik Midelfort's work is representative of those which locate the
impetus for the witch craze at the low end of European society.
Arguing that, even at its worst moments, the churches in southwestern Germany—both Catholic and Protestant—supported the
craze only ambivalently, Midelfort claims that the witch primarily
served the needs of peasant culture. The call for witch hunting issued
from popular pressures: the peasant majority needed to locate scapegoats for the pain and suffering of plague, famine, or other disasters.

His model example is Balingen in Württemberg where, in response to the town's devastation by fire in 1672, the search for a scapegoat led the townspeople to take matters into their own hands and stone a suspected witch when the Oberrat (the Superior Council in Stuttgart) would not act.[30]

Contrasting with Midelfort's "bottom-up" theory of witch hunting is Christina Larner's work. Representative of "top-down" theories of the craze, Larner's analysis indicates that witch hunting was a ruling-class activity aimed at social control.[31] Specifically, witches were pawns in the struggle between secular and church authorities for control of the Scottish countryside. In a game of "who is the godliest of them all" the church and state struggled for authority,[32] tossing the bodies of witches between them and blurring the lines between sin and crime.

Larner's thesis echoes those of Peter Brown and R. I. Moore. Brown argues that "sorcery beliefs may be used like radio-active traces in an X-ray: where they assemble we have a hint of pockets of uncertainty and competition in a society increasingly committed to a vested hierarchy in church and state."[33] Moore, who focuses on the development of a persecuting society in the Middle Ages, claims that European society defined itself and established its borders by engaging in persecution of Jews and lepers.[34] Larner's analysis extends Brown and Moore's theses to the Reformation: it was not the masses who found a voice for their protests against societal uncertainties and cruelties in the courts; rather, it was the courts who found their voice and reason for existing in hunting the masses for witches.

Larner notes that, in the battle for control of the geographical, cultural, and moral borders of Scotland, the state increasingly had the upper hand. Indeed, while it was possible to prosecute a witch under the old machinery of the church, that witch prosecution in Scotland was "conducted throughout under those parts of the machinery of social control which were entirely new" is notable. The statute of 1563 centralized the administration of the Witchcraft Act and extended the authority of the Privy Council in witchcraft cases.[35] The new machinery, once in place, moved only slowly at first. In 1583 the General Assembly of the Church complained to the King that incest, adultery, and witchcraft were not being punished. In 1591, however, the Privy Council rocketed into action and appointed commissions to examine witches. The Privy Council's license to hunt witches lasted until 1597, when the relegated powers were restored to the King (James VI) and witch hunting entered into a period of decline.[36] Despite the efforts of the church to proceed with witch hunting, it was not until the 1620s that the Privy Council interested itself in witchcraft cases again, as part of a general reassertion of its authority.[37] There was a brief lull in the 1630s, a time of plague and famine.[38] But witch hunting entered into a new panic phase in the 1640s, a period which coincided with tension between church and state over their respective boundaries. Again, as in 1583, the General Assembly of the church chastised Parliament for its inaction against witches. The Privy Council established commissions to hunt witches, and witch hunting moved forward on a rising tide until the witch hunting machinery of the state ground to a halt under Cromwell.[39]

Crucial to Larner's thesis that witch hunting was a ruling class activity among institutions competing for social control is her analysis of the role landowners played in the witch hunts. Landowners, rather than ministers, requested most of the commissions and conducted most of the witch trials.[40] Clergy participated in this structure in two ancillary ways. First, the Kirk session functioned as a policing force for local landowners. Appointed and paid by the landowners, the ministers—though nominally of the landed class themselves—stood midway in social structure as a mediating force between landowners and peasants.[41] Second, the ministers facilitated preliminary searches for witches and served as witnesses at their trials.[42] But in each case, the power lay with the landowners and not with the church. Thus, the rise and fall of witch hunting in Scotland is traced by Larner, first, to the structure of centralized authority—the Privy Council-and to its inclination in any particular time to prosecute witches and, second, to the authority of the landowners who, through commissions, carried out the work of the Privy Council.[43] These two groups—council and landowners—hunted witches in order to establish and reinforce their jurisdiction over the countryside. By contrast, the moral and religious fervor which the church directed against witches expressed itself in ways that, though visible, were largely inefficacious. Religion may have accompanied witch hunting, but other social and economic agendas defined it.

Larner's discussion of the dynamics of power played out between the Privy Council, the landowners, and the church offers intriguing prospects for understanding the integration of theologies of gender in the discourse of the witch trials. Suggested by her work is the possibility that, in their struggle to be the primary institution of social control, both the church and the state exploited the ambiguity about gender roles expressed in the differences between pre-Reformation and Reformation theologies. The power of the church and state to impose a particular ideology on women was not just the power to impose that ideology on women's minds. Rather, they forced women to embody the ruling ideology. Applied to the witch trials, the metaphor of "writing the body" well describes this power: in the course of the craze, an underlying fifteenth century text—engraved on women's bodies in terms of lust, weakness and greed—was covered over with a new sixteenth century text, that of responsibility and adulthood. Throughout the craze, old and new texts were inscribed and reinscribed on women's bodies as church and state vied to scratch out a final and definitive sentence that would confirm their sovereign control over the society. Through torture and trial, ideological conformity, which allowed female responsibility only within the context of a patriarchal system of female submission, was engraved on women's very bodies.

Representative of a centrist position, falling between theories advanced by Midelfort and Larner, is Joseph Klaits' work. Klaits argues that interpretive frameworks that emphasize the role of popular pressures in the witch craze and those that highlight the interests of the educated elites in the craze are not mutually exclusive. Klaits blends interpretive models and suggests that witch hunting impulses both "trickled down from the society's leaders" and "rose upward on a tide of popular anxieties."[44] The witch, as scapegoat, served both groups.

For Klaits, the decisive factor in the witch craze, from the side of the educated and politically powerful, was an atmosphere of spiritual reform. That the masses of Europe were being Christianized for the first time is demonstrated by the preoccupation of the clergy with the values and habits of the peasant folk in the countryside.[45] As religious evangelism became increasingly preoccupied with issues of sexuality, the witch appeared as the figure of deviant sexuality on whom evangelistic fervor focused.

Klaits' thesis is influenced by the work of Richard Kieckhefer. Kieckhefer, whose work focuses on preconditions of the witch craze established during the late medieval period, has argued that a conjunction of popular belief in sorcery with a demonology created by a learned culture laid a foundation for the worst excesses of witch hunting. The superimposing of the language of diabolism on that of sorcery "added fuel to an already blazing fire."[46] Specifically, because charges of diabolism embellished charges of sorcery, the discourse of the elite was directly responsible for the craze of spiraling accusations and increasingly harsh punishments. Sorcery—the weapon of the socially powerless when illness, love affairs, quarrels, and communal inhospitality placed them at odds with their neighbors—was elevated in diabolism. Diabolism was used by the devil and his legions in the battle for the souls and bodies of an entire people. Where the sorcery called for reparations—the lifting of curses, the return of "borrowed" property, reciprocal apologies and protestations of forgiveness—diabolism summoned forth all the powers of the state to do battle with evil. At stake was not the harmony of a single community or clan, but the survival of human society itself.

Moreover, if, at first, demonology served primarily to "translate" popular belief into the language of the educated, it was not without its own popular appeal. With a theory of demonology in place and a legal system prepared to bring all its powers to bear against the devil, when demonological theory "trickled down" to the masses, after gestating among the elite in the fourteenth and fifteenth centuries, the zeal to exterminate devil-worshipers knew no limits. Beliefs in sorcery and in demonological witchcraft mingled to form one virulent world view. With their fears joined, popular and learned cultures required and hunted down a virtually endless supply of victims.[47]

Extending Kieckhefer's analysis of the links between popular sorcery and demonological theory, Klaits attributes the reformers' preoccupation with issues of deviant sexuality—as expressed in their demonological theory—to the association of sexuality with the core of human identity. The decisive proof of successful inculcation of Christian values and habits required by the reformers issued upon one's ability to demonstrate one's liberation from the wiles of Satan, specifically one's freedom from the perverse sexuality of Satan's servants.[48] Moreover, because the reformers believed that women were weak and particularly prone to the devil's seduction, clerical suspicions rested more and more on them, feeding an increasingly virulent hatred of women among the clergy.[49]

At the same time as spiritual reform was advancing across the countryside, the ordinary masses upon whom the clergy turned their attention had their own problems. Social unrest created great insecurities. The search for scapegoats came to rest upon lonely, poor women who "touched the subconscious anxieties of the villagers who saw in their isolation the worst fears they had for themselves."[50] Fed by the misogynistic suspicions of the reformers, these frustrations precipitated the witch craze.

Thus, for Klaits, witch hunting served a dual purpose. For the masses it focused anxieties, provided an explanation for their miseries, and "took the people's minds off their troubles."[51] For the clerical elite, it served to validate the authority structure of society and to give vent to their misogynistic feelings about women. Moreover, because an "unanticipated side effect" of legal reform was the creation of a judicial apparatus conducive to witch hunting, both the masses and the elites found their search for scapegoats efficaciously channeled.[52] With their fears and hopes joined in the courts, the clergy and lay peasantry could accomplish their objectives: the witch trials both publicly demonstrated the truth of the reformers' vision and power—bringing the battle with the devil to a decisive conclusion—and provided the cathartic release the masses had been seeking.

Klaits can be applauded for attempting to honor the complexity of the witch craze by meshing "top-down" and "bottom-up" interpretive frameworks into a single theory of reciprocal influence and for wanting to accord to religion a more central role in the witch craze than have Midelfort and Larner. Nevertheless, his own efforts remain marred by oversimplifications. When Klaits identifies the religious reformers as the vehicle by which the sentiments of the masses and the machinery of a judicial elite were brought together in one place, with explosive results, he misreads key factors in that sequence of events. First, mitigating Klaits' notion of misogyny as the driving ideological force behind the witch hunts are Larner and Karlsen's demonstrations that misogyny characterized the dominant, pre-Reformation ideology of gender, but not that of the Reformation. Second, notwithstanding the fact that the Reformation did Christianize the European countryside, Klaits errs in imputing vast power to the church. Because Klaits fails to integrate the rise of the nation state into his portrait of the Reformation, he ascribes to the clergy more power than they actually had. He makes religion central to the witch hunts, but only because he oversimplifies the notion of religious power, reducing it to clerical politics and mistakenly designating the clerical vision as the dominant ideology. If religion did have a decisive impact on witch hunting, it cannot be for the reasons Klaits cites.

If Klaits overestimates the power of the church, he underestimates the power—ideological and practical—of the courts. Larner's analysis of the conflict between the lay courts and the clergy suggests that Klaits' vision of the role of the courts in the witch hunts is naïve. Her thesis is both more specific in its documentation and more comprehensive in its scope than Klaits': witch hunting was not the "unanticipated side effect" of the new judicial system but was, in fact, integral to the development of that system.

Finally, even if we amend Klaits' portrait of the elite to include judicial as well as clerical elites, his portrait of the peasant masses remains problematic. If Klaits' interpretive framework is to stand, we need to know not only the discourse of the elite which trickled down to the masses, but also the discourse of the masses which rose up as a tide toward the elite. Klaits identifies the frustrations of the masses without giving thóse frustrations voice. Cited only as "primordial fears," the anxieties of the peasant folk remain amorphous.[53] If the language of fear expressed by the peasants was more than or other than the language of the elite that had trickled down to them, Klaits must show us this language, but he does not. Thus, in a variety of ways, Klaits fails to meet his own challenge to honor the complex dynamics of witch hunting by setting them in a single, integrative framework.

The Witch in Mythic Perspective

Current analyses of the witch craze, reflecting broader trends in historical scholarship dealing with religion, make a laudible advance over earlier treatments. None, in discussing the religious backdrop to the craze, argue that belief in witchcraft was a superstition held by the masses of which they were finally freed by the great wisdom of eighteenth-century humanism. Not only have scholars realized that such an interpretation betrays a kind of ethnocentrism that distorts our understanding of the sixteenth and seventeenth centuries, but, more to the point, research on the witch craze has shown that the witch craze ended with beliefs about demonology still intact among both the educated elite and the peasant masses. According to recent scholarship, witch hunting did not end because persons ceased to believe in witches. Instead, state and church machinery needed to hunt witches fell into disarray, no longer able to discriminate reliably between real witches and those falsely accused.[54] Nor did the state and church need to use this machinery. The eighteenth century would see each utilize different strategies of legitimation. Moreover, the eighteenth century saw the resolution of earlier ambiguities about gender roles. Freed from the borderline status women had had in the flux of pre-Reformation and Reformation times, women were secured within the walls of a newly-created domestic sphere. Confined safely in that moral preserve,[55] women in the eighteenth century did not pose a substantive threat to the social order, and reason to suspect them of witchcraft declined dramatically.

Despite their advances over earlier scholarship, I wonder whether the analyses I have summarized here have replaced earlier theories about religious superstition with understandings of the role of religion in the witch craze that are substantively more adequate than those which preceded them. I want to argue that the strength and weakness of each theory hinges on the adequacy of each theory's notion of the witch as scapegoat.

The common thread linking the typologies of the witchcraft craze that I have summarized is the figure of the scapegoat. According to Midelfort, a changing court system played into the hands of those bent on finding a scapegoat for various natural and social disasters. For Larner, the witch, a scapegoat for various natural and social disasters, played into the hands of a political institution bent on legitimating itself. Finally, opting for a centrist position, Klaits locates the scapegoat at the juncture of new institutional structures where peasant anxieties were channeled into mass panic.

For the most part, each account does advance our understanding of the witch craze. Moreover, I believe that, of the lot, Larner, who invests most in an ideological interpretation of witch hunting, offers the most persuasive analysis. After all, Midelfort and Klaits must see the court's change to the inquisitorial trial, so advantagous to the prosecution of witches, as serendipitous. How convenient that, just when the peasants and/or the clergy needed a scapegoat, court procedure changed to accommodate them. By contrast, Larner describes a straightforward convergence which acknowledges the changing political forces of Europe: that the court changed is precisely why witches were hunted. Witches were what the court generated in the state's process of self-legitimation.

Despite my appreciation of current research, the theories cited here remain problematic. The category of the scapegoat, I argue, does eventually betray the adequacy of these accounts to the phenomenon of witch hunting. In seeking to understand the scapegoat phenomenon, current research does, for the most part, reduce these women to anonymous cogs in the machinery of a persecuting society.[56] So also does it reduce religious language about witches to a coded language of politics and protest. Neither tack does justice to the scapegoat. Instead, these modes of analysis continue to participate in an historical amnesia that perpetuates the victimization of the women condemned as witches and leaves their persecutors unchallenged. They are inadequate to the goals of feminist scholarship.

In my efforts to take the charge of feminist history to heart, I want to demonstrate this thesis by appeal to René Girard's *The Scapegoat.* Notwithstanding two qualifications — *The Scapegoat's* relevance for my thesis is based on extrapolations, and Girard's paradigmatic scapegoat is not the witch of the sixteenth and seventeenth centuries but the Jew persecuted for causing the plague in the fourteenth century— I seek to demonstrate that Girard's work does speak to feminists in significant ways, advancing the goals of our scholarship.

With Girard's study in mind, let's consider one possible record of a witch trial and execution, written by an accuser, which states that "a woman was executed because she caused the plague."[57] From our current vantage point as feminist scholars, we make two judgments about such a record of an historical event: we are sure that the woman did not cause the plague and we believe she really was executed. On what basis do we confidently and blithely disregard an account of a day that recorded the execution of a woman for witchcraft? The author/accuser says both that the woman caused the plague *and* that she was executed. Why do we want to split in two a text that records an execution, affirming one half and denying the other? Apparently, the frame of contemporary analysis is one in which we feel that we must either do such violence to the text or let the text continue to do violence to the victim of persecution, thereby affirming the accuser's charge and justifying his murderous actions.[58]

Our intentions are honorable, but we may not achieve our aims. Why? With Girard, I suggest that, in our current efforts to vindicate the woman accused of witchcraft, we also deny her access to a truth that is crucial to condemning her persecutor: the persecutor's own belief in the witch's guilt. That belief can not be challenged if we, on behalf of the victim, rend the unity of the persecutor's text. Instead, we must go back inside the text, inside the mind of the persecutor, there to break the pattern of violence from the inside.

We advance the cause of the innocent victims of persecution only if we ourselves set out on the trail of persecution that the prosecutors were too naïve to cover.[59] Because the traces of that truthful trail are left in the mythic language that the persecutors used to justify their acts, ideological analyses which bypass that language or replace it with codes of political and ideological intrigue may make sense of the witchcraft craze, but only at the price of leaving the victims of witchcraft craze where their persecutors left them—unvindicated—and the way of persecution still open for future use.

When we ask of a woman accused of witchcraft, "Was she who her accuser said she was?" and, by appeal to analyses such as those reviewed in this essay, gather evidence, put her on trial again, and pronounce her innocent, we play a strange game with truth. We say that the accuser, speaking as he did about demons, diabolic contagion, and the witch's pact, was unaware of what he was doing: he was frustrated by changing marriage patterns, confused by economic instability, angered by plague and famine, and embattled over claims to political turf. Angered, frustrated, confused, and embattled, he picked out an innocent woman and killed her. What we do not say in all of this language is that this man was a persecutor. The reason we do not say this is that the language of witch *persecution* had only one home: sacred myth.[60] If we alter the language of witch persecution, severing it from its roots in myth in order to render its meaning in other terms, we will never unpack the meaning of the word "scapegoat."

That epithet "scapegoat," which so often characterizes our gut-level reaction to the witch craze, needs more careful analysis if it is to become a well-grounded claim. Ungrounded, the category of scapegoat is highly vulnerable to expropriation to the interests of ideological analysis, where its meaning, impoverished and malnourished, will always be under threat of complete extinction. To properly ground the notion of the scapegoat we must locate its place within a persecutory structure and locate the roots of that structure in the sacred. Only then may it be possible to overthrow the persecutor rather than to overthrow only the persecutor's texts, as has current witch craze scholarship.[61]

What then is the structure of persecution? Girard cites four stereotypes of persecution. In referring to these characteristics as stereotypes, he leads us away from the pejorative connotations which attend the use of that word. He reminds us that a "stereotype" is a metal cast used in printing that enables the unvarying and fixed reproduction of an original image or pattern. Hence, stereotypes of persecution are persecutory patterns advanced by the type in fixed and unvaried reproduction across cultures and centuries.

The first stereotype of persecution locates it only in times of crisis. Plague, famine, floods, institutional collapse, all qualify as crises. Such crises announce the obliteration or collapse of hierarchical or functional differences between persons.[62] Violence attends this eclipse of culture: persons at both ends of the social scale—kings and women or children—are the most vulnerable to violence. Sexual and religious crimes abound: rape, incest, bestiality. Ultimately, a small number of persons are determined to be extremely harmful to the whole of the society.[63]

A second stereotypic accusation is needed to bridge the gap between this very small group, sometimes a sole individual, and the social body. What is at stake is order: of the community and even the cosmos.[64] How could one small group or individual carry the powers that could destroy a much larger whole? Images of contagion provide the answer and fuel the stereotype: the individual's capacity to cause illness or to use poison augments his or her powers to destroy and closes the gap between the individual and the society as a whole.[65]

The crowd's choice of victims points to the third stereotype: the victim is generally characterized by a lack of difference from his or her accusers.[66] This stereotype seems at first counter-intuitive. Aren't persons persecuted because they are different—a Jew is not Christian, a woman is not a man, a spinster is not married? Certainly, the many feminists who have understood the problem of woman's oppression in terms of her role as the "Other," utilizing a typology of "dualism," have identified the "woman-problem" as an issue of difference. But Girard's claim is not as surprising as it might seem. He offers the example of the physically disabled person. Disability is disturbing to others, not because of its difference, but because of its impression of disturbing dynamism.[67] Life goes on, in difference, giving the lie to the exclusive truth of our own lives. What bothers heterosexuals, ethnic and religious majorities, and the able-bodied about those who are different—gays and lesbians, ethnic and religious minorities, the disabled—is the potential they see in those persons "for the system to differ from its own difference, in other words not to be different at all, to cease to exist as a system."[68] The relativity, fragility, and mortality of one's own small world is put into relief by the one who is different. Different persons are reproached not for their difference, but for being not as different as expected, and in the end for differing not at all.[69]

In failing to respect "real" differences, those who are "not-different-enough" incur others' anger and bring down upon themselves the fourth stereotype of persecution: the violence that would defend difference by inscribing that difference on the bodies of the indifferent and, in so doing, would create the expiatory sacrifice which could return the whole community to order. Torture and death complete the persecutory structure.[70]

Two stories highlight Girard's analysis of these stereotypes of persecution. In one story a Jewish woman is depicted contemplating two pigs to whom she has just given birth. In another story, a woman has intercourse with a dog and gives birth to six puppies. Her tribe banishes her and she is forced to hunt for her own food. The first story is from a 1575 German text describing the Jewish proclivity for witchcraft. The second is from a myth of the Dogrib people. Each story bears the marks of the stereotypes of persecution. The background for each, explicit in the former and implicit in the latter, is crisis. The women flaunt cultural distinctions, engaging in bestiality. Because they are women, they bear essential victim marks. Moreover, they fail to differ as they should from others, inviting the scapegoat mechanism. That lack of difference is implicit in the former story of the Jewish woman[71] and explicit in the Dogrib myth, which tells us that the puppy children are really human, having the ability to remove their fur coats at will and reenter the world of human society.[72]

With these examples, we begin to see that lines separating history and myth are arbitrary in stories of persecution.[73] The structure of persecution is indifferent to such categorical distinctions, for the Dogrib and the author of the 1575 German text are telling the same story. Yet we want to read them differently. We want to deny the mythic meaning of the story from Germany and translate its meaning, following rules of witchcraft interpretation represented by scholars such as Midelfort, Klaits, and Larner.

Why do we refuse myth? For those who are not scholars of religion, that question is easily answered. We live in a society that has a highly impoverished view of myth. That myths found and shape a people's common life—their memories, their hopes and dreams, their fears, their ultimate concerns—is virtually forgotten. But, how do we, scholars of religion, answer this question? The hermeneutics of our discipline allows a far greater appreciation of myth. We know that the standard of truth in myth is not empirical correctness, but its life-founding potential: a myth is true if persons live by it and find their hopes, fears, memories, and values carried forth by it. Thus, for scholars of religion, the question of myth-refusal in analyses of witch persecution is not so easily answered. In the earnestness of our quest to recover the memories of the victims of the witch craze, have we shied from an embrace of myth that would bring us too close to the accuser? Is that why we have forgotten the lessons of our discipline? Perhaps another of Girard's stories will jolt our memory:

> Harvests are bad, the cows give birth to dead calves; no one is on good terms with anyone else. Clearly, it is the cripple who is the cause. He arrived one morning, no one knows from where, and made himself at home. He married the most obvious heiress in the village and had two children by her. All sorts of things seemed to take place in their house. The stranger was suspected of having killed his wife's former husband, who disappeared under mysterious circumstances and was rather too quickly replaced by the newcomer. One day the village had had

enough. They took their pitchforks and forced the disturbing character to clear out.[74]

Girard places his tale in the Christian middle ages: it is a tale of persecution if ever there was one. But others may recognize another, much older story, the myth of Oedipus. Again the lines between myth and history blur.

What can we make of Girard's play with the boundaries of myth and history? His comments suggest that scholars of the witch hunts need to grant to the stories of the witches the respect ethnologists grant the Dogrib.[75] We need to listen to those stories the way we listen to the myth of Oedipus. To listen to them in that way is to understand persecution in a way that only myth preserves because only myth carries forth the stereotypic structures of persecution intact. Only myth reveals persecution as the dark lining of religious beliefs and practices. Only myth holds together in one frame, for better or worse, both violence and the sacred.

To really listen to a witch's story is to return to the rite of sacrifice of the scapegoat.[76] But when we think of the ceremony, the priest, and the expiation of sins, we must go farther with our reflection on the scapegoat than does current scholarship. If we are to enter the mythic world of the witch craze, we have to enter a persecutory structure in which the victim—the chosen scapegoat—was not only responsible for public disasters but also *was capable of restoring, symbolizing, and even incarnating order.*[77] We have to honor the power of the victim to do what scapegoats do.[78]

But that we will not allow. We may, in attempting to enter the sixteenth-century mind, suspend our disbelief and see that, for her accuser, the witch was responsible for public disasters in some mythic, larger-than-life sense. However, we balk at giving to the witch the power her persecutor gave her. We cannot see that, so great a power did the witch have that, for her accuser, extraordinary measures were required to capture and channel it for the good. We do not understand that, in accord with that belief, her accuser had to torture a woman accused of witchcraft in order to gain her confession, which was the required "proof" of her power, and that he had to execute her in order to demonstrate that those powers had been successfully foiled. Not understanding, we fail to listen to the accuser's tale of violence and overlook the clues he gives us about the place to which he has taken his victim. Not heeding his words, we leave the scapegoat where her accuser has left her—unvindicated—and do not seize the opportunity to wrest from his hands the key that would unlock the persecutory structure so that the scapegoat could be freed.

Our resistance to according to the scapegoat the power her persecutor granted her, nowhere more evident than in recent scholarship's silence and puzzlement before the violence which announced the witch's power and marked the struggle against it, highlights our incapacity to read the mythic elements of the witch craze. Challenged by the need to integrate accounts of violence into its theoretical perspectives on the witch craze and denied the old "superstition" argument by its advocacy of non-ethnocentric analyses, current scholarship uses two strategies in order to make sense of torture and execution. Neither strategy acknowledges adequately the mythic home of the persecutory structure.

Scholarship informed by the first strategy documents the elements of persecution – descriptions of torture and transcripts of confessions – recorded by the witches' accusers. Observations count as explanations. Thus, Larner, Midelfort, and Klaits dutifully record the importance of the witch's confession for the accusers and those accusers' stated opinion that torture alone would free the witch from her enslavement to the devil. Repeatedly, each scholar also notes the persecutors' oft-stated claim that the witches told the truth under torture. Midelfort highlights it.[79] Trevor-Roper documents it, observing that the accusers' confidence in the mechanism of torture to extract the truth from the accused outlived their confidence in the existence of witches.[80] Klaits also comments about the "genuine concern" the accusers had for the accused. He underlines the sense of integrity he reads in their statements: they truly believed in the guilt of the women they prosecuted and were absolutely confident that those women, confessing under torture, told the truth.[81]

The inadequacy of this strategy of analysis to the violence of the witch hunts becomes apparent when we note the surprise of the historians before their recorded observations. Midelfort is not the only one to be confounded by the persecutors' repeated claims that the witches told the truth under torture. Others seem equally bemused.[82] The absolute confidence of the accusers in the truthfulness of the accused appears irrational to the contemporary mind. For us, that witchcraft suspects would lie under torture to save their lives is as comprehensible as it was apparently incomprehensible to the accusers of their day. Seeking to better explain the beliefs they have observed in the accounts of the witch hunters, scholars turn to a second strategy.

Observing no rationale in the external discourse of the witch persecutors, they appeal to masters of unstated discourse: the psycholo-
gists. Aware that they are testing the limits of their methodologies,
each is circumspect in his or her conclusions. Noting that her views
are "just speculation," Larner muses about the "psychological
cleansing effect on a community" of the witnessed execution of
witches.[83] She also describes the witch's confession as "the triumph
of the state in the battle for minds." Confession demonstrated the
accused's sentience: correct ideological commitment (to the state)
was accompanying ideological re-education (in the interrogation and
trial).[84] In a similar vein, Klaits compares the interrogators of witches
with the interrogators in the Stalinist purge trials. He suggests that,
immersed in an ideology and committed to a higher good, each
looked to confession as a necessary step in "ideological reeduca-
tion."[85] Further, comparing the judicial application of torture in the
sixteenth and seventeenth centuries with the use of the lie detector
in today's judicial system, Klaits suggests that, in each case, absolute
confidence in the ability of the machinery to extract the truth leads
to the willing confession of the accused. In the earlier time, accusers
believed the women they tortured were telling the truth because the
women themselves came to believe they had been rightfully accused.
Providing a contemporary parallel is the case of Peter Reilly, a
Connecticut teenager who was accused of murdering his mother in
1973. Repeatedly interrogated by lie detector, Reilly came to believe
in his guilt. He confessed to the murder, even though subsequent
investigations established his innocence. Such "brainwashing" or
"thought reform," according to Klaits, whether located in the witch
hunts or in contemporary judicial practices, appeals to the same
"psychological dynamics."[86]

While not wholly disavowing these explanations, I suggest that the
theorists considered here would do well to entertain a greater variety
of explanations. An appeal to psychology may once again entail a
distorted "translation" of the witch hunting dynamic. Is Peter Reilly's
lie detector ordeal the closest parallel to the witch's ordeal by torture
on the rack? Our study of the persecutory structure of myth suggests
not. The witch's closest kin is not Reilly, but the sacrificial victim of
an earlier time. The key dynamic of her ordeal is not "brainwashing,"
but "ritual." And the end to be achieved is not psychological catharsis
or successful thought reform, but the expiation of sin and the restoration of cosmic order.[87]

This mythic model accounts best for an accuser's confidence in the
truthfulness of his victim's confession. How could he believe that the

witch had real power, that all initiative came from her, that she alone was responsible for the cure as she was for the sickness in the society?[88] Proper neither to political ideology nor to psychological thought control, the logic of his discourse expressed the sacred and appealed to a pattern of causality proper to it: expiatory powers had to cross the threshold of death, and only that which was transcendent and supernatural could cross that line. The witch had to be made to appeal to powers beyond herself if, at her death, those powers were to live on after her. The woman accused of witchcraft had to be tortured and killed because only those actions followed the trail of death and summoned the transcendent powers of good to do battle with the powers of evil, so that sin could be vanquished and godly order reign again.[89]

Our resistance as scholars to a mythic reading of the witch craze is well-intentioned. We think that if we acknowledge any power in the women charged as witches—which in myth we must acknowledge—they will cease to be victims unjustly accused. We think that if we listen to their stories as their persecutors did, even for a moment, we will bloody our own hands. But Girard's work has led me to consider a different possibility. If we resist the mythic reading of the witch craze, the persecutors cease to be persecutors. If the persecutors were not persecutors, then the women whose innocence we wish to proclaim were not victims. We must read the tales of persecution through the eyes of the persecutors because in their eyes alone lies the full structure of persecution undisguised.

We will not save the victims of the witch craze by snatching them from the grip of history to put them on trial again and to declare them the innocent victims of economic unrest, political change, or psychological manipulation. Rather we will save them by putting their persecutors on trial. Such a trial will be as much or more the task of the theologian as of the historian or sociologist, for the primary texts of human sacrifice are religious texts whose myths plumb the human spirit at its innermost depths. To truly challenge the persecutors we must challenge them there, on their own turf. Only then will we be able to name the myth that has fueled their violence and to free the victims from the place of their incarceration. Only then will we know enough about the persecutor—his motives and his weapons—to condemn him. We must turn to myth if we are to grasp the persecutory structure at its roots and break its power.

If we are to protect victims of scapegoating we must examine why the religions of the West and, in particular, Christianity, have been religions of sacrifice. We must find out why humans live by myths of persecution, and we must seek alternate myths to live by that can account for crisis, anomie, and angst in human life without need for the expiatory sacrifice. Vigilance is required to protect victims: past and potential. But we practice vigilance on behalf of victims only by turning toward the persecutors and the myths by which they live, seeking them out wherever they may be. Ironically, faithfulness to history is possible only if we embrace myth.

Can we do this? The forces of amnesia which make it impossible for us to read the mythic elements in our own past history are very strong. Indeed, Girard's further examples of our confusion before the arbitrary distinctions between myth and history must give us pause. Girard notes that, in the middle ages, physicians first resisted the notion that the plague could be spread through physical contact with the disease. They opposed quarantines of plague victims. Did they harbor naïve superstitions about the workings of disease? Were they stubbornly clinging to current theories of the plague because they had some ideological investment in the status quo? No; Girard applauds their enlightenment. The theory of contagion smacked too much of a persecutor's prejudice not to be suspect. The physicians saw in the contagion theory of the plague the structure of persecution. For the idea of contagion to be accepted by physicians it had to be freed from the persecutory structure. That time awaited the nineteenth century.[90]

With this example, the lines between myth and history blur once again. The physicians, we would say, misjudged the parameters of myth. They made a mistake. But are mistakes always made in the same direction? Consider the witch trials. In a movement directly opposed to that taken by the physicians who viewed the new theory of the plague as part of a persecutory myth, and sought real causes elsewhere, we deny to the witch craze its mythic elements, confident in the truths offered by the social sciences. Both we and the medieval physicians have denied myth in order to make room for truth. The medieval physicians got it backwards. Have we?

My confidence in the adequacy of the discourse of the social sciences to the phenomenon of witch hunting has been profoundly challenged by Girard, who writes that, "if our ancestors had thought in the same mode as do today's masters, they would never have put an end to the witch trials."[91] Challenged by his vision, I believe increasingly that, only if feminist scholars look at the mythic investment humans have in the scapegoat, will we be able to come to terms with the terrors of persecution and recount our foresisters' stories *in memoriam*.

Even so, when we work to redeem the past on behalf of a future freed from terror, we must wonder whether, in our own time, if humans have not lost the capacity to create scapegoats, we may have lost the capacity to recognize that a scapegoat who has no expiatory powers is no scapegoat. Unless we can confront that problem directly, and take its lessons to heart, the risk of new witch hunts remains high, for we continue to live in a society that searches for scapegoats and lives by the scapegoat myth, even as its capacity to recognize myth fades from memory.[92] The tragedy of this cultural amnesia may be not only that our society can recognize everyone's scapegoats but its own.[93] The tragedy may be also that, no longer at home in a mythic universe, yet still in need of scapegoats, those who live in the modern age, more than those of the past, may seek them in evermore virulent ways.

NOTES

1. The quote in the title is attributed to Cotton Mather in 1693, as cited in John Putnam Demos, *Entertaining Satan: Witchcraft and the Culture of Early New England* (New York: Oxford University Press, 1982) 313. The epigraph is from René Girard, *The Scapegoat*, trans. Yvonne Freccero (Baltimore: The Johns Hopkins University Press, 1986) 99.

2. Adrienne Rich, "Resisting Amnesia: History and Personal Life," in *Blood, Bread, and Poetry: Selected Prose 1979-1985* (New York: W. W. Norton & Company, 1986) 146.

3. Phyllis Trible, *Texts of Terror: Literary-Feminist Readings of Biblical Narratives* (Philadelphia: Fortress Press, 1984) 3.

4. The total number of executions will never be known because many records have been lost or destroyed and surviving records do not always list names. Some merely record that "many witches were executed." While estimates vary widely, low estimates range from 100,000 to 500,000 victims. The exact figures are of little consequence. As Christina Larner notes, "the conspicuousness of witch hunting is not modified by precise figures, and there is a sense in which failure to be appalled by the hunt on the grounds that we know that on a particular day we are talking of twenty-seven witches rather than two hundred would be a distortion of its own." In Christina Larner, *Enemies of God: The Witch-Hunt in Scotland* (Baltimore: Johns Hopkins University Press, 1981) 16.

5. Larner 193.

6. H. C. Erik Midelfort, *Witch Hunting in Southwestern Germany, 1562-1684* (Stanford: Stanford University Press, 1972) 67.

7. Midelfort 104-6.

8. Midelfort 187-88.

9. Joseph Klaits, *Servants of Satan: The Age of the Witch Hunts* (Bloomington: Indiana University Press, 1985) 56–57.

10. The majority of victims were women. Of the twenty percent of victims who were male, most were charged with additional crimes (e.g., heresy) and not exclusively with witchcraft, or they were relatives of women accused of witchcraft and were guilty by "contagion" or association (Larner 91–94; Midelfort 95; Demos 60–62). Demos devotes one chapter (36–56) to the case of John Godfrey who, as an exception to the general rule, was accused of being a witch for reasons similar to those cited in the cases of females accused of witchcraft. Godfrey's life was characterized by extreme rootlessness: no parents, no spouse, no children, no property. Demos speculates that homosexuality may have been a factor in his persecution.

11. Midelfort 182.

12. Midelfort 184.

13. John Hajnal, "European Marriage Patterns in Perspective," in *Population in History*, eds. D. V. Glass & D. E. C. Eversley (Chicago: Aldine Publishing Company, 1965) 101–147.

14. Midelfort 184.

15. Carol F. Karlsen, *The Devil in the Shape of a Woman: Witchcraft in Colonial New England* (New York: W. W. Norton & Company, 1987) 101.

16. Karlsen 102.

17. Karlsen 214–18.

18. Keith Thomas, *Religion and the Decline of Magic* and Alan Macfarlane, *Witchcraft in Tudor and Stuart England,* as cited in Klaits 87–94.

19. Klaits 90.

20. Klaits 91.

21. Demos 298–300.

22. Larner 101.

23. Larner 102.

24. Larner 102.

25. Karlsen 120–25.

26. Karlsen 141.

27. Karlsen 144.

28. Karlsen 154–55.

29. Karlsen 181.

30. Midelfort 190.

31. Larner 64.

32. Larner 73.

33. As cited in R. I. Moore, *The Formation of a Persecuting Society: Power and Deviance in Western Europe, 950–1250* (Oxford: Basil Blackwell, 1987) 141.

34. Moore 146–48.

35. Larner 58.

36. Larner 71.

37. Larner 72.

38. Interestingly, Larner finds the lull inexplicable; others, noting that

plague and famine years often alternated with witch hunting years and that the latter provided a scapegoat mechanism for the tragedies of the former, would find the lull quite explicable (Demos 386, Midelfort 70–73).

39. Larner 73–75.

40. Larner 40.

41. Larner 56.

42. Larner 106–7.

43. Larner 88.

44. Klaits 150.

45. Klaits 60.

46. Richard Kieckhefer, *European Witch Trials: Their Foundations in Popular and Learned Culture, 1300–1500* (Berkeley: University of California Press, 1976) 105.

47. Kieckhefer 73–92.

48. Klaits 76–77.

49. Klaits 72.

50. Klaits 102.

51. Klaits 103.

52. Klaits 132, 176.

53. Klaits 176.

54. Midelfort 196; Larner 73–75.

55. Karlsen 180–81, 255–56.

56. Some aspects of Karlsen and Larner's work are an exception to this rule. More than the other scholars mentioned, they affirm the engagement of women accused of witchcraft in the struggles to determine their fates, countering their anonymity and object-status. Each notes that some women assumed the role of witch as a strategy of aggression in a social context in which they were powerless otherwise. Because a poor, peasant woman, angered and frustrated by her lot in life, could, in acts of sorcery against her neighbor, recoup on wrongs done to her, the trials were a forum for women's discontent (Larner 94–96; Karlsen 244). Even so, because both Karlsen and Larner must locate the women accused of witchcraft on an ideological grid in which men defined and used women for their own political, economic, and social aims, Karlsen and Larner's efforts to identify with the women they study, in the end, do serve only to reinscribe the women accused of witchcraft as anonymous "cogs" in the machinery of a persecuting society.

57. That Girard begins his exploration (Girard 4) of the scapegoat with an analysis of texts that record the execution of a scapegoat is most suggestive to my own thesis. The adequacy of current analyses of witchcraft persecution is precisely a question of the adequacy of scholars' interpretations of the documents generated by the accusers which record the witch craze. The text with which I begin my reflections is an imaginary one that captures the essence of a typical complaint against women accused of witchcraft and parallels, in a different century, a fourteenth-century text of Guillaume de

Machaut cited by Girard. In that account, a number of Jews were executed because they caused the plague.

58. Girard 8.
59. Girard 8.
60. Girard 38.
61. Girard 10.
62. Girard 12–13.
63. Girard 15.
64. Girard 15.
65. Girard 16.
66. Girard 22.
67. Girard 21.
68. Girard 21.
69. Girard 22.
70. Girard 45–57.
71. The third stereotype of persecution—the lack of difference of the victim from his or her accusers—identifies an important element in anti-semitism. The dynamics of anti-Jewish prejudice, stemming from the first century of the Christian era, as recorded in the New Testament, are highlighted by this typology. The differentiation of Christianity, as a separate religion, from Judaism, was very much an intra-familial debate: Judaism and Christianity were two children, born of the same parent: pre-rabbinic religion (see Rosemary Radford Ruether, *Faith and Fratricide: The Theological Roots of Anti-Semitism* [New York: The Seabury Press, 1974] 62). Thus, in the story of the Jewish woman cited here, the dynamics of her persecution are traced, not to her "alienness," but to her lack of difference from those who would secure the boundaries of their altogether fragile world at her expense.
72. Girard 48–49.
73. Girard 47.
74. Girard 29.
75. Girard 53, 96.
76. Girard 40.
77. Girard 42.
78. Girard 44.
79. Midelfort 142.
80. H. R. Trevor-Roper, "The European Witch-Craze of the Sixteenth and Seventeenth Centuries," in *The European Witch-Craze of the Sixteenth and Seventeenth Centuries and Other Essays* (New York: Harper & Row, 1967) 122.
81. Klaits 150.
82. Midelfort 142; Trevor-Roper 121; Klaits 149.
83. Larner 115.
84. Larner 184.
85. Klaits 84.
86. Klaits 155–58.
87. Girard 55. Note: Supporting this analysis is Larner's own observation

(Larner 113) that witch executions were preceded by a day or days of fasting and sermons. Prior to the modern era and the ascendance of medical discourse, fasting was meaningful within the context of religious discourse. That, apart from her brief observations, Larner has remained silent about the meaning of fasting suggests that she may have recognized the inadequacy of her mode of analysis to this phenomenon. Were she to have integrated fasting into her theory—witch hunting was the instrument of ideological education of a state bent on legitimating itself—she might have said that "a hungry stomach is a stomach attentive to the state's message." By contrast to that impoverished analysis, in the context of Christian myth, for centuries, communal fasting had united a people before God. Partaking of a ritual of communal penitence and invoking divine power, in fasting, a people made themselves vulnerable before God in order that, through suffering and loss, they might induce God's blessings. Fasting thus served the drama of the witch execution by preparing people for the sacrificial act that would banish evil and return God's people to their covenant with God.

88. Girard 43.
89. Girard 44, 94.
90. Girard 19.
91. Girard 99.
92. Girard 50.
93. Girard 41.

The Contributors

ALICE BACH, the editor of *Union Seminary Quarterly Review*, is the author of more than twenty books for children and young adults. Two of her novels have been named *NY Times* Best Book of the Year. Since returning to school in 1985, she has written a series of mystery novels about a pair of high-school girls solving crimes with computers, as well as a novel, *He Will Not Walk With Me* (Delacorte, 1987). *Moses' Ark: Stories from the Bible* (Delacorte Press, 1989), written with J. Cheryl Exum, was a Best Book of 1989 of the American Library Association. She and Professor Exum have written a second volume *Miriam's Well: Stories about Women in the Bible* to be published by Delacorte in 1991. A doctoral student in biblical studies at Union, her research involves literary strategies for reading biblical and pseudepigraphic texts.

J. CHERYL EXUM, associate professor of Hebrew Bible at Boston College, has published widely in the area of biblical criticism. She is the editor of several volumes on biblical poetics, including *Reasoning with the Foxes: Female Wit in a World of Male Power* (*Semeia* 42) with J. W. H. Bos, and *Signs and Wonders* (Scholars Press, 1989). She is at work on a literary study, *Arrows of the Almighty: Tragedy and Biblical Narrative*, forthcoming from Cambridge University Press.

CAROLE R. FONTAINE is associate professor of Hebrew Bible at Andover Newton Theological School. She is the author of *Traditional Sayings in the Old Testament: A Contextual Study* (Almond Press, 1982). Her poetry and artwork have appeared in the journal *Anima*. She is presently at work recovering ancient women's voices for a full-length study *Holy Torch of Heaven: Goddesses, Queens and Ordinary Women*, of which her article in this volume is a part.

DORY PREVIN is a lyricist, novelist, composer, and performer. She is the author of two autobiographical works *Midnight Baby* and *Bog-Trotter*, and several musical plays, among them *Mary C. Brown and the Hollywood Sign*. One hears in her songs and her books a woman's voice, sometimes brave, sometimes scared to be alone, always exploring—from the star-stained heights to the depths where the iguanas live. She is currently at work on a volume of short stories.

MARTHA J. REINEKE, assistant professor of religion in the Department of Philosophy and Religion, is also director of women's studies at the University of Northern Iowa. Her essay in *Union Seminary Quarterly Review* is part of a larger work, *Life Sentences: Reflections on Women, Violence, and the Sacred*. Other recent works that form background to this larger work include "Life Sentences: Kristeva and the Limits of Modernity," *Soundings* LXXI, no. 4, 439–461; and "This is My Body: Reflections on Abjection, Anorexia, and Medieval Women Mystics," in *The Body as Social Text*, ed. Catherine R. Burroughs and Jeffrey Ehrenreich (1990).

ELLEN ROSS is assistant professor of the History of Christian Life and Thought at Boston College. Ross has recently published articles in *Downside Review* and *Listening*. Her major research interests are in the fields of medieval mysticism and contemporary feminist theology.

MARY ANN TOLBERT is associate professor of New Testament and Early Christianity at Vanderbilt University Divinity School. She holds graduate degrees from the University of Virginia (English literature) and University of Chicago (biblical studies). She is the editor of *The Bible and Feminist Hermeneutics* (*Semeia* 28) and the author of *Sowing the Gospel: Mark's World in Literary-Historical Perspective* (Fortress, 1989).